T5-AWK-561

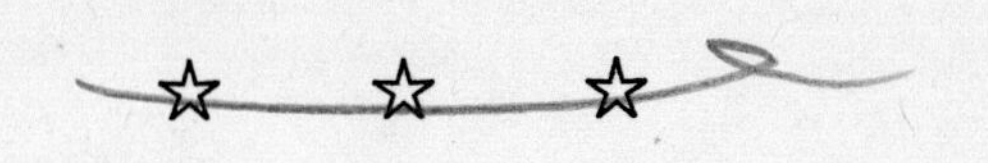

PRINT
BLURB
& BIO
ON
THIS
PAGE

"I do solemnly swear . . ."

"I do solemnly swear..."

☆ ☆ ☆

THE STORY OF THE
PRESIDENTIAL INAUGURATION

by Milton Lomask

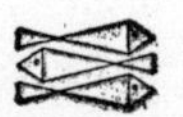

ARIEL BOOKS
Farrar, Straus & Giroux
New York

Library of Congress catalog card number: 66–11686
Published simultaneously in Canada by Ambassador Books, Ltd., Toronto
Printed in the United States of America by H. Wolff, New York

Second Printing, 1968

For the members of
the Children's Book Guild
of Washington, D.C.

Contents

"I do solemnly swear . . ."

I

From Washington to Lyndon B. Johnson

☆ ☆ ☆

On the morning of Thursday, April 30, 1789, the voices of men in earnest debate echoed in the spacious red-white-and-blue Senate chamber on the second floor of what for the time being was the Capitol of the United States, the recently remodeled sandstone building then known as Federal Hall at the corner of Broad and Wall streets in New York City. Earlier, the twenty-two Senators and fifty-nine Representatives comprising the first Congress under the Federal Constitution had convened in joint session. Under consideration was a question in ceremonial procedure. Later that day General George Washington was to take his oath of office as the first President of the United States. When the time came for him to deliver his inaugural address,

3

should the members of Congress, who would be listening to him, stand or sit?

Those in favor of standing pointed out that when the king of England spoke from the throne, the members of the lower house of Parliament, the Commons, always stood. They contended that in a country where no titles of nobility were permitted, all citizens were commoners and should act accordingly.

It was the argument of men who had been born and who had grown to manhood as Englishmen. To be sure, they had rebelled against the mother country. They were independent of her now, but, baffled as to how to proceed with their own as yet untried government, they still looked to her for ways of doing things.

Those who favored sitting while the President gave his address went to the same source for a different argument. They pointed out that when the English sovereign spoke from his throne the members of the upper branch of Parliament, the Lords, remained seated. In a country where one citizen was as good as another, they contended, all were entitled to behave like Lords.

The vigorous debate came to an abrupt close when someone observed that twelve o'clock, the hour at which Washington was scheduled to take his oath, was almost at hand and the committee appointed to bring him from his New York home ten blocks away had not yet left the building. The members of the committee, four Senators and four Representatives, were dispatched at once.

They had no sooner departed than another crisis arose. The committee charged with planning the inaugural ceremonies had decided that the President-elect should take his oath by placing his hand on a Bible. But what Bible? None could be found in Federal Hall.

This problem was solved by tall, black-garbed Chancellor Robert R. Livingston, who as presiding judge of the most important court in the state of New York had been selected to administer the presidential oath. Livingston rushed off a messenger to the meeting rooms of the nearest Masonic lodge. When half an hour later Washington stood on the balcony of Federal Hall above Wall Street and repeated the words of the oath after the Chancellor, his right hand rested on a Bible borrowed from St. John's lodge and opened to the last chapter of Genesis. And when, having bowed to the wildly cheering throng in the street below and on the rooftops of the neighboring buildings, he returned to the Senate chamber, the problem of republican etiquette so fruitlessly debated that morning was solved without a word. As the monumental old soldier stepped into the big room with its starred and canopied ceiling, the people awaiting him there spontaneously rose and remained standing throughout the twenty minutes required for the delivery of his address.

☆ ☆ ☆

In this manner was the first President of the United States inducted into his demanding office. From that day to this, from George Washington to Lyndon B. Johnson, thirty-five men in all have taken the presidential oath on fifty-three different occasions.

For no two of them have the details of the occasion been exactly the same. The Constitution of the United States lays down no program for the presidential inaugural. The

Constitution as it stood in Washington's day contained only one relevant paragraph. It directed that before assuming his duties, the President-elect must promise to execute them properly. The Constitution as it now stands contains one further relevant paragraph—a statement in the twentieth amendment, ratified February 6, 1933, that the date on which the President is sworn in, previously established as March 4 by act of Congress, is now January 20.

All the other activities we have come to associate with the installation of a President—the revels and the hullabaloo, the salvos and the ovations, the balls, the concerts, the choruses and the galas, the sometimes seemingly endless parades in the afternoon and the fireworks in the evening—all these are the product not of law but of custom and tradition.

Because the inaugural rite is so varied, it may be likened to a vast mirror. In it we see ourselves, our changing attitudes, interests, hopes, and fears.

To a degree, every President writes his own program. Although other men planned the first inauguration, Washington succeeded in placing his stamp upon it. One of the characteristics of his subsequent administration was the care with which he honored the letter and spirit of the Constitution, but in the opening phase of his first inauguration he deviated from the great charter.

The Constitution prescribes the form of the oath. "I do solemnly swear (or affirm)," the President-elect is required to say, "that I will faithfully execute the Office of President of the United States, and will to the best of my Ability, preserve, protect and defend the Constitution of the United States."

These were the words uttered by Chancellor Livingston. Washington repeated them, but at the end he added a phrase of his own. "So help me, God," he said. Ever since, every President has concluded the taking of his oath with these four words, except Theodore Roosevelt. Harboring some serious doubts about the existence of any being higher than himself, Teddy altered the traditional closing by saying instead, "And so I swear."

The President-elect, be it noted, may "swear to" or "affirm" the contents of his oath. For him, to swear is to direct his promises to God. The significance of this form of the oath was brought out by Abraham Lincoln in his first inaugural address in 1861, when he warned the rebelling states of the South that he must do all in his power to bring them back into the Union because the oath he had just taken to preserve the Union was "registered in Heaven."

The President who affirms merely expresses his sincere determination to carry out his promises. So far only one, Franklin Pierce of New Hampshire, has chosen to affirm rather than to swear. The young, handsome fourteenth President never explained his reasons for selecting this form of the oath, but they can be deduced from the circumstances surrounding his inauguration on March 4, 1853.

On the previous January 7, tragedy had befallen Pierce and his wife. They were en route from Boston to their New Hampshire home, when the train on which they and their son Bennie were riding hurtled from its tracks into the gully at the foot of the embankment. The President-elect and his wife were scarcely injured, but eleven-year-old Bennie, hopelessly caught in the wreckage, died before their eyes.

Pierce never got over it. Intensely, even morbidly religious, he could never shake off the conviction that his son's death under these cruel circumstances was God's way of punishing him for his sins. Perhaps his decision to use the word "affirm" in taking the presidential oath was based on the belief that he was too unworthy a man to direct his promises to God.

Washington, at his first inauguration, initiated another custom when he leaned forward and kissed the Bible after completing his oath. The book borrowed for the ceremony and still preserved in the archives of St. John's Masonic lodge in New York was a King James version of the Bible, the translation most commonly used in the Protestant churches of English-speaking countries.

Subsequent Presidents have used the King James, with two exceptions. At all four of his inaugurations, Franklin Delano Roosevelt took his oath on an old Dutch Bible, version unknown, that had been in his family since 1670. As the first Roman Catholic to be elected to the Presidency, John Fitzgerald Kennedy took his on a Douay Bible, the translation commonly used among English-speaking Catholics.

At three inaugurations, no Bible was used. Vice President Chester Alan Arthur was in New York City when on September 19, 1881, word reached him that President James Abram Garfield, shot by a disappointed office seeker on the preceding July 2, had died at a New Jersey seaside resort. When no Bible could be found in Arthur's Manhattan home, it was decided to proceed without one rather than leave the country, agitated by the assassination, without a President for so much as another minute. When Arthur returned to Washington, the swearing-in ceremony was repeated at the Supreme Court, this time with a Bible.

Equally tense circumstances prevailed when Vice President Theodore Roosevelt was elevated to the White House by the assassination of President William McKinley. Roosevelt was mountain-climbing in the Adirondacks of Vermont when on the afternoon of September 13, 1901, he learned that McKinley, wounded a week before, was dying in Buffalo, New York. That night the Vice President was on his way, traveling the first thirty-five miles on a speeding buckboard wagon along dangerous mountain roads. It was 1:30 the following afternoon before he reached Buffalo, to find that McKinley was dead. When no Bible could be found at the home to which he was taken to be sworn in, it was decided to go ahead without one—again because speed in filling the Presidency was believed to be of the essence.

Vice President Calvin Coolidge was at his father's farm in Vermont when shortly after midnight on the morning of Friday, August 3, 1923, he was awakened by a messenger from the nearby village of Plymouth and informed that President Warren Gamaliel Harding had succumbed to a heart attack in San Francisco. A kerosene lamp lighted the room of a plain New England home as Coolidge's father, a notary public, administered the presidential oath. The room was scarcely large enough to hold the eight individuals hastily summoned as witnesses. Outside a score of neighbors, peering through the door and windows, watched the proceedings with awed eyes. A Bible lay on the table, but it was not used. Coolidge explained that it was not the custom in Vermont to swear on Holy Writ. Back in Washington a few days later, he, like President Arthur, repeated the ceremony with a Bible.

Any public official can administer the presidential oath, but custom has assigned this function to the Chief Justice of the United States. At Washington's first inaugural, the Supreme Court, which the Chief Justice heads, was not yet in existence. At his second, the oath was administered by an associate justice, but since the accession of John Adams in 1797 all regularly elected Presidents have been sworn in by the head of the high court. Of the eight Vice Presidents lifted to the Presidency, only one, Andrew Johnson, received his oath at the hands of a Chief Justice. When at Dallas airport on November 22, 1963, Lyndon Johnson succeeded to the office vacated earlier that day by the murder of John Kennedy, Federal Judge Sarah T. Hughes of the Northern District of Texas became the first woman to administer the oath.

☆ ☆ ☆

An American humorist has noted that an inaugural address is not required by law but that "Washington gave one and no succeeding president has been able to resist the temptation." As a matter of fact, the eight Vice Presidents-become-Presidents confined themselves to a few impromptu remarks. Of these informal speeches, that of Lincoln's successor, Andrew Johnson, appears to have been the longest; that of Coolidge, the shortest. At the conclusion of his first swearing-in, Coolidge assured his Vermont neighbors that he could handle his new job. "I think I can swing it," said Silent Cal.

Of the forty-five formal inaugural addresses to date, only

one—Washington's second, on March 4, 1793—approached to this delightful brevity. Delivered in the Senate chamber of Congress Hall in Philadelphia, whence the seat of government had been moved from New York in the autumn of 1790, it consisted of four sentences and 135 words.

It set no precedent. Washington's successor, John Adams, also speaking in the Senate chamber of Congress Hall, relieved himself of a thirty-minute oration, one third of which consisted of a single sentence of 700-plus words.

The longest inaugural address was given on March 4, 1841, from the east portico of the permanent national Capitol in Washington. The speaker was William Henry Harrison. For two hours, six thousand spectators in the plaza in front of the Capitol endured the lash of a chill northeast wind while the ninth President pelted them with generalities. Then as now, the nation had problems, but President Harrison gave them short shrift. Much of his wordage consisted of quotes from the writings of the Roman proconsuls, the gentlemen chosen to govern the provinces of ancient Rome during her imperial heyday. The address would have been even longer and more ornate, had it not been for Daniel Webster. Requested to edit it, the great New England statesman, as he later revealed to the landlady of his Washington boarding house, made life easier for Harrison's audience by "killing off seventeen proconsuls."

☆ ☆ ☆

The original date of the presidential inauguration, March 4, was chosen by the last Congress to sit under the Articles of Confederation, the document by which the United States was governed from March 1, 1781, until the Constitution took effect on March 4, 1789. It is believed March 4 was chosen because an examination of the calendar for the next fifty years or so revealed that date fell on Sunday less often than any other. When inauguration day does fall on Sunday, the public ceremonies are held on Monday. On these occasions some Presidents-elect, rather than leave the country without a Chief Executive for twenty-four hours, have taken their oath twice—first at noon on inauguration day, when the term of the incumbent President ends and a new term begins; second, during the festivities of the following day.

Except for Washington's brief appearance on the balcony of Federal Hall in 1789, all of the early inaugurations were held indoors. This custom was broken on March 4, 1817. The incoming President was James Monroe, and the circumstances surrounding the last-minute shift of place is an example of the often observed tendency of Clio, the muse of history, to imitate Thalia, the muse of comedy.

During the closing days of the War of 1812, three years earlier, the interior of the national Capitol in Washington had been gutted with fire by the invading British. Pending restoration of the Capitol, Congress was meeting across the street in the red structure, first known as Brick Capitol, that stood for generations on the land now occupied by the Supreme Court building.

The committee in charge of Monroe's inauguration planned it for the chamber of the House of Representatives in this now-vanished landmark. The failure of these plans dated back to 1814, when, after moving into Brick Capitol, Congress appropriated $5,000 to furnish its temporary quarters.

Somehow the Senators got their hands on this money first. By the time they had purchased some bright red leather chairs for themselves, the remaining funds were barely adequate to supply the members of the other House with wooden kitchen chairs. The Representatives had been seething ever since. When the committee on arrangements decreed that for Monroe's first inauguration the Senate's handsome chairs would be moved into the House chamber and placed across the front, their anger became rebellion. Fortunately for a nation then on the threshold of what historians call the Era of Good Feeling, the Speaker of the House in 1817 was the Great Compromiser, Henry Clay of Kentucky. A squabble was averted when Clay announced that the House chamber could not be used for the inauguration at all because the floor was too weak to support the anticipated crowds. Clay's fears were purely diplomatic, but the committee on arrangements seized upon them with relief. Monroe took his oath and delivered his address from a wooden platform on the grounds in front of Brick Capitol.

Eight years later his successor, John Quincy Adams, took his oath and delivered his speech from the unfinished east portico of the National Capitol. Ever since, this has been the traditional spot for the high points of the inaugural ceremony.

☆ ☆ ☆

Not that all newly elected or newly re-elected Presidents have begun their four-year terms at this location. At his fourth inauguration, in 1945, Franklin Roosevelt stood on the south portico of the White House to take his oath and deliver a brief speech—twenty-six sentences, 560 words—to the 9,000 people gathered in the snow-covered gardens below him.

On at least three occasions, bad weather has forced the ceremonies inside. In 1909 a blizzard that smothered the Federal City in ten inches of wet snow and gave it the stormiest inauguration day in history persuaded William Howard Taft to take his oath and deliver his address in the Senate. Taft himself was willing to brave the March winds, but he moved the ritual inside in deference to the frail health of Chief Justice Melville W. Fuller. Riding in the inaugural parade in an open landau pulled by four horses, the newly installed President likened the slush to lemon ice and said he had already earned his first day's salary.

So common is bad weather on the great day that among the citizens of Washington, snow, rain, sleet, freezing temperatures, and ill winds are frequently spoken of as "inaugural weather." A viewer of the ceremonies on March 4, 1841, described the day as "a regular marrow-searcher." For the incoming President, William Henry Harrison, it was fatal. Proudly refusing to place an overcoat between himself and the sleet-laden winds, the sixty-seven-year-old hero of the War of 1812 caught a chill that a month later became pneumonia. On April 4, "Old Tippecanoe" was dead, the first President to die in office.

Although a drenching rain pounded the outdoor ceremonies for James K. Polk in 1845, his aristocratic wife insisted on carrying the ostrich-plume fan she had chosen for the event. Polk was more practical. Mindful of the fate of "Tippecanoe" Harrison, he submitted to a rubdown by the servants and changed his clothes the minute he reached the White House after his swearing-in.

Ulysses S. Grant's second inauguration was the coldest on record, only slightly above zero. At the ball in the evening, the celebrants danced in their overcoats and hacked at frozen oysters and champagne. A steady downpour attended the ceremonies for Benjamin Harrison in 1889. As Old Tippecanoe's grandson read his inaugural address, his predecessor, Grover Cleveland, held an umbrella over his head. Streams of dirty water splashed off the manuscript, and during the forty-five-minute parade that followed, Harrison warmed himself with generous draughts of beef tea.

A few weeks after Washington's first inauguration, a formal dance was given at the executive mansion in New York. Shortly after his second, there was a similar affair, to which only members of Congress were invited. People spoke of these gambols as inauguration balls, but the ball was not opened to the public as an official part of the ceremony until 1809, when James Madison became the fourth President and his "fine, portly, buxom" Dolley—to quote Washington Irving—became number one in the long line of the capital city's great political hostesses.

Contrary to a legend which gallantly credits Dolley with dreaming up the inaugural ball, the idea originated with a group of young men who had organized and made themselves managers of Washington's first dancing assembly. Tickets for the ball were made available at the bar of the hotel where it was held. Theoretically, anyone could buy them. In actual practice, the guests were selected by the dancing-assembly managers. Exactly 400 attended. Some students of the lighter side of American life say this happenstance was in the mind of Ward McAllister, for twenty years the director of the social affairs of the rich in New York, when in 1888 he declared that there were "only four hundred people" in that city worth knowing—thus giving birth to the custom of speaking of high society as the Four Hundred.

The first inaugural ball was held at Long's Hotel, a popular hostelry then standing across from the Capitol on ground now occupied by the multi-staired entranceway to the main building of the Library of Congress. The President and his lady arrived early and stayed late. Dolley wore "a sumptuous yellow velvet gown . . . and a Parisian turban with bird-of-paradise plume." Her husband wore the same clothes in which he had been sworn in at noon. According to eyewitnesses, a good time was had by all, with the possible exception of the guest of honor. Madison was eighteen years older than his Dolley. As the evening wore on, and the windows resisted being opened and were broken to let a little air into the crowded ballroom, the President confided to a friend that he would much rather be "home abed."

Like all of the trimmings gradually incorporated into the inaugural ceremony, the ball has grown more elaborate with the passing years. One such affair was enough for Madison; but the festivities for Martin Van Buren in 1837 were climaxed by two balls, those for William Henry Harrison by three, and those for John F. Kennedy in 1961 by five. At one of the most elegant, the ball concluding the second swearing-in of William McKinley in 1901, a hospital set up at the entrance to the Pension Building, where the ball was held, was kept busy throughout most of the evening.

It was also at Madison's first inauguration that what has become the most eye-filling facet of the ceremonies, the parade in the afternoon, took its official place on the agenda. The route traversed by Madison and his little escort, a troop of cavalry and some militia companies, has never varied substantially.

Today, as then, the parade takes form in the vicinity of the Capitol, mostly along New Jersey Avenue to the south. Getting underway shortly after the President finishes his address, it moves north past the east portico of the Capitol as far as Constitution Avenue. There it turns left to travel for five blocks due west along Constitution. At Fourth Street Northwest it bears to the right into America's most celebrated street, Pennsylvania Avenue. Onward it rolls in a northwesterly direction, past the National Gallery of Art, past the simple marble block erected in front of the National Archives to the memory of Franklin Roosevelt, past the other buildings of the Federal Triangle, past the headquarters of the Coast Guard and the District Building, as far as Fifteenth Street. Here it turns right, proceeding for three blocks on Fifteenth alongside the Treasury Department. Finally it turns left, again into Pennsylvania, to march past the White House through what has been known since Civil War days as the Court of Honor. On its right, as it enters this last lap of its route, is Lafayette Park. On its left stands the reviewing stand occupied by the incoming President, the outgoing President, their families and numerous dignitaries.

☆ ☆ ☆

The parade, as could be said of all the other aspects of the great day, reflects both the temperament of the incoming President and the current preoccupations of the country.

Negroes were in the line of march for the first time at Lincoln's second inauguration. A score of bands blared "Dixie," the anthem of the South, while 50,000 people along the parade route rejoiced at their country's imminent delivery from the horrors of civil war. Twenty years later, at the first inauguration of Cleveland, a contingent of Confederate soldiers walked in the parade for the first time. Spectators who saw in their presence a sign that the bitterness of the Battle Between the States was gone were disillusioned when later the "Rebels" went yipping through downtown Washington, pilfering shops, breaking windows, taunting the police, and creating damage estimated at $10,000.

Nineteenth-century parades were dominated by fife and drum corps, by herds of livestock from the frontier, by bands of what one reporter described as "America's quadrennially rediscovered Indians." In the cavalcade that accompanied James Buchanan from the Capitol to the White House in 1857, large floats representing the states and various American institutions were used for the first time.

Twentieth-century parades, like the century itself, have been characterized by innovations. The procession for Herbert Hoover in 1929 was the first to have an airborne section—five airships and fifty-five airplanes. The airborne "marchers" got off the ground without difficulty, but there was so much fog and rain that the five airships lost sight of each other soon after their take-off from New Jersey. Only twenty-seven of the planes got through to Washington; the

cloud cover over that area was so thick, spectators on the ground caught only infrequent glimpses of what was going on overhead; and the crew of the lead airship *Los Angeles* listened on radio to a parade they could not see. The parade for John F. Kennedy featured another hallmark of the century, truck-mounted missiles capable of carrying nuclear warheads.

The longest parade took place during the second inauguration of Dwight D. Eisenhower, in 1957. Leaving the Capitol about 2 p.m. in 54-degree weather, unusually warm for Washington in January, the paraders were still moving through the Court of Honor after darkness fell. A gray mongrel dog marched the entire route, and was immortalized by a newspaper photographer who picked up the hound in his lens as he trooped past the reviewing stand, with General Eisenhower standing at attention in the background.

The parade always draws a crowd. The 750,000 on hand for Eisenhower's second inauguration set the record as of that date, but a million people lined the route for Kennedy's parade, and 1,200,000 for Lyndon Johnson's. The shadow of President Kennedy's tragic death lay over the Johnson parade. So rigorous were the precautions taken to protect the newly sworn-in President that the tribal dancers of a participating Indian band were required to remove the stone heads from their arrows.

New elements in the parade are not the only twentieth-century additions to the inauguration. Another is the gala, introduced at the third inauguration of Franklin Roosevelt, in 1941. Usually held two nights before the great day, and staged by stars from the entertainment world, the gala is advertised as a salute to the President, although its main purpose is to raise money to help defray the ever mounting expenses of the inauguration.

☆ ☆ ☆

Practically every inauguration yields one or more "firsts." John Quincy Adams was the first President to take his oath in long pants. Van Buren was the first to call for his predecessor (Andrew Jackson) at the White House, thus establishing the practice of the two Presidents—the old and the new—riding to and from the Capitol together. The custom is for the outgoing President to sit on the right en route to the swearing-in, the incoming President to occupy that side on the trip back to the White House. Having begun life six years after the signing of the Declaration of Independence, Van Buren was the first President to be born an American citizen.

William Henry Harrison was the first President to arrive in Washington by train for his inauguration. John Tyler, who succeeded him a month later, was the first Vice President to take over the Presidency. Polk's inaugural address was the first to be relayed to the country (actually only as far as Baltimore) by telegraph. Pierce was the first and so far the only President to deliver his address from memory. Harding was the first to ride to and from the Capitol in an automobile. Coolidge's second inauguration was the first to be broadcast. Truman's second—his first as an elected President—was the first to be televised.

America's fluctuating tastes in music can be traced in the offerings that have accompanied the induction of nearly every President. The marine band, usually set up in front of the platform at the Capitol, has been included in the program since 1841. At Cleveland's first inauguration, in 1885, the concert, now traditionally held on the night before the big day, was given official status. The marine band, the National Symphony Orchestra, and Fred Waring and his Pennsylvanians have been among the instrumentalists to perform at this concert. From time to time, vocal numbers, usually sung by opera stars, have been added. At Teddy Roosevelt's 1905 inauguration, a chorus of one thousand voices joined the Marine Band at three inaugural concerts. Patriotic songs and some of the noisier moments of opera predominated. Franklin Roosevelt leaned to grand opera, Eisenhower to light opera, and Kennedy broke ground by selecting for the concert a program of serious music by American composers.

For generations, those parts of the inauguration for which Congress holds itself responsible were arranged by a committee made up of Senators. In 1897, President-elect McKinley requested that the members of the House of Representatives be allowed to participate. Since then, a joint Congressional committee has been appointed. For each inauguration, Congress appropriates a fund to underwrite the costs of the actual swearing-in ceremonies and to supply the capital city with extra police and other additional municipal services.

The money thus provided by the taxpayers amounts to only a fraction of the total costs. All the trappings of the inauguration—the parade, the balls, the concerts, and the like—are underwritten by a guaranty fund supplied by business firms, individuals, and organizations. Supervising the expenditures from this fund is a mammoth committee, the chairman of which is appointed by the President-elect. The civilian inauguration committee, which consists of thousands of people, is divided into many subcommittees. The members of these groups take care of most of the preparations, a task that begins at least three months before inauguration day and continues for at least three months after.

The contributors to the guaranty fund are repaid at least in part from the proceeds raised by the sale of seats in the grandstands along the parade route, of souvenirs, and of tickets to the various entertainments. In only one inauguration in this century—Hoover's—have these proceeds been sufficient to repay all the contributors in full.

Hoover wanted no parade but was overruled by popular demand. Much the same fate befell his expressed wish that the ceremonies be simple and quiet. His Vice President, Charles Curtis, had Indian ancestry. On inauguration day, 1929, Washington was noisy with celebrating Indians and colorful with tepees set up in the plaza in front of the Union Railroad Station and on the Mall at the foot of the Washington Monument.

☆ ☆ ☆

To turn from the mechanics and the glitter of the inauguration to its more serious aspects is to face the question of what it is all about.

In the opening of his inaugural address, President Kennedy told the crowd before him: "We observe today not a victory of party, but a celebration of freedom. . . ."

Actually, both elements mentioned by Mr. Kennedy are found in every inauguration.

The induction of the President is indeed a "celebration of freedom." Once again it presents to the world the spectacle of a free people freely placing in the hands of one of their number, an individual chosen by themselves, the power and the majesty of their government. Nothing like this had ever before taken place in the world when George Washington stepped onto the balcony of Federal Hall in 1789. No government so begun has ever endured as long.

But at the same time the inauguration is a "victory of party," a rally for the members of the political faction whose presidential candidate has won.

Call it a celebration of freedom or a victory rally, no American ceremony is fraught with greater significance. None is of interest to a greater number of people. The thousands of Fourth of July orations made in this country have left no more trace behind them than the air into which they were spewn. But the first official words of a newly elected or newly re-elected President, his inaugural address, is awaited with anxious expectation, listened to or read with concentrated attention, commented on around the world, and lavishly recorded and analyzed in the books of history.

The main reason for this intense interest is that every inauguration marks a step in the development of the American nation. The inaugural festivities outline our history. They dramatize our problems, illuminate our weaknesses and strengths, our failures and successes. They indicate the direction in which we are moving. Sometimes they even lift a little the curtain beyond which lies the future.

When the central figure of this combination celebration and rally stands forth to take his oath, America is one kind of country. When four years later his term ends, it is always a different kind.

Sometimes the change is small, as during the slow-moving years of the Era of Good Feeling, when James Monroe sat in the White House. Sometimes, as in the troubled days of Lincoln, it is very great, even cataclysmic.

As time moves on, we come to speak of the Presidents involved in these great changes, these historical watersheds, as turning-point Presidents, and of the ceremonies which ushered them into office as turning-point inaugurations.

And it is to the drama and the meaning of some of these more crucial inaugurations that the subsequent chapters of this book are devoted.

2

The experiment begins

☆ ☆ ☆

GEORGE WASHINGTON

On the clear, mild morning of April 16, 1789, the first farmer of Virginia, dressed for travel in blue broadcloth and black boots, stood for a few minutes on the piazza of his house, from which point his gaze could take in most of the several miles of Potomac River that bordered his plantation to the south.

George Washington was bidding goodbye to his beloved Mount Vernon. To these spreading acres he had retired in 1783 after eight years as the military leader of a war in which he had known a dozen humiliating failures for every success, a thousand anxious hours before the final moment of victory at Yorktown.

During the intervening years, he had only once absented himself from this happy spot for any substantial length of time. That was in the summer of 1787, when for four scorchingly hot months in Philadelphia he had presided over the convention that had drawn up the Constitution of the United States. Subsequently, that blueprint for "a more perfect Union" had been ratified by the states, and under the election procedures prescribed in its pages, he had been named to his new government's highest office.

Two days before, a messenger from Congress had brought him the official notice of his unanimous election. Now he must journey to New York to be the central figure of the first presidential inauguration.

How he felt as he stepped into his waiting carriage about ten o'clock that April morning, we know from his own lips: "like a culprit . . . going to the place of his execution." First in War, Washington had no desire to be First in Peace, but given his character, his love for his country, and the overwhelming evidence he had received in the recent elections of what his countrymen expected of him, he had no choice.

For the reluctance, amounting to dread, with which he set forth to take up his new tasks, he had many reasons.

One was the simple desire to remain where he was, to continue enjoying the repose of Mount Vernon after the grueling years of war.

Another was his health. At fifty-seven, the firm look of his large and erect frame belied the growing weakness of a once seemingly indestructible physique.

Still another was a financial predicament he had no way of resolving save by staying at Mount Vernon. As Commander-in-Chief of the Continental Army for eight years, he had received no salary, and as President he intended to accept only enough money to take care of the expenses necessary to the performance of his job. During the war his plantation had suffered from inadequate management, and since the war it had been the Mecca of thousands of curious visitors, many of them uninvited but all of them hungry. To discharge his debts and take care of his expenses in getting to New York, he had been obliged to borrow close to $24,000, at six percent interest, from a wealthy citizen of Alexandria, Virginia.

Finally, there were his sincere doubts about his ability to give life and form to Article 2 of the Constitution, where the powers and duties of the President were so skimpily enumerated. Trying to understand the blueprint of a new government, as the American author Carl Van Doren has written, is like trying to understand a score of music. The untrained person cannot begin to hear in his head the complex sounds indicated by the written notes. And in 1789 *nobody* was trained in the conduct of the Presidency of the United States because no office exactly like it had ever existed before.

Ahead of General Washington as his carriage rolled northward was a task as formidable as the one he had undertaken fourteen years earlier when the Continental Congress had placed him in charge of the Revolutionary forces. What he did as President would establish precedents for generations to come. It could even make or break the office—and by extension, the government to whose helm he had been elected.

Two men accompanied him. One was Charles Thomson, who, as secretary to Congress, had brought the official news of his election to Mount Vernon. The other was tall, ruddy-complexioned Colonel David Humphreys, the General's long-time confidential aide.

The ride to New York could be made in five days, but Washington's journey to his first inauguration took eight, broken as it was by stopovers for celebrations in his honor.

At Alexandria it was a public dinner, lengthened by after-dinner speeches, to which the President-elect listened with a grave face and to which he replied with grave words.

At Georgetown, on the Potomac, then one of the major shipping centers of Maryland, it was a parade to the clamor of church bells and the clatter of musketry.

Crowds filled the streets of Baltimore. At the Pennsylvania border the General and his party were met by Governor Thomas Mifflin and a troop of cavalry, come to escort them all the way to Philadelphia. There were festivities on the way to that historic city and in the city itself, and more festivities at Wilmington, in neighboring Delaware.

At Trenton, in New Jersey, a triumphal arch composed of thirteen flower-decked pillars straddled the road along which the President-elect approached. In front of it stood thirteen white-clad maidens, each with a flower basket on her arm. As Washington appeared, astride a white horse brought along for such events, the young women broke into song, the words of which they accompanied with appropriate actions:

Virgins fair and matrons grave,
Those thy conquering arm did save,

Build for thee triumphal bowers;
Strew, ye fair, his way with flowers!
Strew your hero's way with flowers.

The concluding phase of the journey—by water from Elizabethtown Point on the Jersey coast to Murray's Wharf on the East River at the foot of Wall Street in New York City—was a crash of sound and a carnival of movement and color. As the resplendidly decorated and especially built barge bearing the General's now much-enlarged party emerged from the Kills between New Jersey and Staten Island, a score of other vessels—barges, sloops, private fishing craft, and gunboats—fell in behind to form a parade across the bay of New York.

Foreign ships anchored in the harbor ran up their flags, fired their guns, and put their crews at attention. Dozens of smaller vessels, putting out from shore, brought crowds of New Yorkers to greet the arriving hero with choral singing and carefully timed huzzahs. According to an eyewitness, even the natives of the bay took part, a school of porpoises surfacing as Washington's satin-awninged barge passed Bedloe's Island to gambol in its wake.

Cannon boomed from Fort George at the southern tip of Manhattan. Practically all of the city's 30,000 inhabitants lined the waterfront from the Battery to Murray's Wharf, where, between two and three o'clock on the afternoon of Thursday, April 23, Washington set foot on the crimson carpet tacked to its steps. From here bands, military units, and thousands of citizens headed by Governor George Clinton of New York escorted the President-elect northward along Queen Street to Franklin Square, where one of the city's finest houses—Number 3 Cherry Street—had been set aside as the executive mansion.

☆ ☆ ☆

Another week passed before Washington was sworn in. The government called into being by the new Constitution was slow in getting underway.

From the beginning, almost nothing had gone quite according to schedule.

The electoral college, the device by which a President and a Vice President are named, was one of the many compromises arranged by the Constitution-makers at the Federal Convention in Philadelphia. Only a few of the delegates favored letting the people of the United States vote directly for the President and the Vice President. Most of them feared that such a system would put too much power in the hands of the people and rely too heavily on their judgment. To reconcile the two points of view, it was decided to let the people vote only indirectly. Each state was to name a group of electors, who, along with the electors chosen in the other states, would cast the actual votes for President and Vice President.

This arrangement still prevails. A citizen's vote for presidential candidate A is not a vote for Mr. A at all. It is a vote for a slate of electors who are either pledged to vote for Mr. A or are believed certain to do so. Each state is entitled to as many electors as it has Senators and Representatives in Congress. The method by which they are chosen is left to the state. At this moment the electors are chosen by popular vote in every state, but in Washington's day and for many years thereafter this was not the case.

As soon as nine of the thirteen original states ratified the Constitution—the number specified by the Federal Convention as enough to give it effect—the Congress of the old government authorized by the Articles of Confederation began making preparations for the installation of the new government. New York was selected as the national capital. January 7, 1789, was named as the day when the electors would be appointed. And on the following February 4 the Electoral College—all of the electors—would cast the decisive ballots. The first Wednesday in March, which happened to fall on the fourth, was named as the day when the new Congress would assemble and the new government take over.

On the first national election day, January 7, the states employed two methods for choosing their electors. In four of them the people went to the polls as they do now, but in six the choice was made by the legislature. Two states, North Carolina and Rhode Island, did not participate, as they had not yet ratified the Constitution. New York ruled that the legislature would make the choice, but when election day arrived, the two political factions in the state's upper house were so embroiled in a long-standing wrangle that the legislature never got around to naming any electors at all.

When a month later the electors cast their ballots, it was found that Washington had received all sixty-nine of the votes for President, but John Adams of Massachusetts, the Vice President-elect, had received only thirty-four votes. The remaining votes for that office had been scattered among ten other candidates.

Meanwhile Senators-elect and Representatives-elect had

been named by the states, and on March 4 the new government took over—or would have, had there been any government to do so.

But there wasn't. On that day, only eight of the twenty-two Senators and thirteen of the fifty-nine Representatives were in New York. March 4 was the day when Washington and Adams should have been inaugurated, but that could not be. The Constitution directs that, having cast their ballots, the electors must mail them to the president of the Senate, who is then required to open and count them in the presence of both Houses of Congress.

Until this action is taken, no individual elected to the Presidency or Vice Presidency can be inducted into office. Since the Constitution specifies that neither House of Congress can do business unless a quorum, a majority of its members, is in the chamber, the handful of Senators and Representatives in New York on March 4, 1789, could do nothing about Washington and Adams.

The situation was no better on the next day. It was not much better a week later. Day after day, for more than a month, whatever Senators and Representatives were in New York climbed to the second floor of Federal Hall, counted the empty seats in their chambers, shook their heads, grunted, and adjourned to the livelier atmosphere of the nearest tavern.

To some extent, this delay on the part of members of the first Congress in getting to New York was due to bad roads after a harsh winter. To some extent, it was due to the apathy that many of them felt for their strange new government. Not until April 6 was Congress able to count the ballots and so officially confirm the well-known results of the national election.

John Adams reached New York on April 21, took his oath, assumed his duties as presiding officer of the Senate, and promptly involved that body in a farcical but turbulent debate.

Adams was of the opinion that before President-elect was inaugurated, some high-sounding mode of address should be invented for him. Did the Senators have any ideas? They had several, or rather the committee appointed to study the matter did.

One proposal was that Washington be addressed as "His Mighty Mightiness." This was too much for rock-faced Senator William Maclay from the backwoods of Pennsylvania. The acid-tongued democrat muttered that well-padded Adams should be addressed as "His Rotundity" and was gratified when a senatorial wag suggested that the President be addressed as "His Excellency" and the Vice President as "His Superfluous Excellency."

The debate shortly evaporated amidst grumbles and laughter, leaving future Americans free, as an amused historian has remarked, to address their chief officer in any way their sense of what is proper or "their political animosities" may direct.

This little scene in the first Senate—no joke to most of the men involved—had unfortunate effects. It strengthened the inaccurate impression held by many then and later that John Adams would have preferred a king to a President. It also tended to downgrade the office of Vice President. Washington was apparently annoyed by Adams's lack of common sense in wasting time on so petty an issue. Previously the General had consistently consulted with Adams on governmental problems; thereafter he did so infrequently. Because Washington tended to ignore his Vice President, succeeding Presidents did the same. It was not until the 1950's that Eisenhower broke with precedent by taking his Vice President, Richard M. Nixon, into his confidence and assigning him to important missions.

Even after Washington finally arrived in New York, his inauguration was further delayed. During the Revolution and the occupation of the city by the British, the building then known as Federal Hall, now the United States Subtreasury, had fallen into decay. The retiring Congress had practically no taxing powers and the new government was penniless, but money enough to put the building in shape—some $32,000—was subscribed by wealthy New Yorkers. On April 23, when Washington reached the city, the remodeling was not quite finished, so the inaugural ceremonies were put off until the following Thursday.

☆ ☆ ☆

Inauguration day, April 30, 1789, dawned gloomily, but by nine o'clock the skies had cleared and a bright and warming sun fell over the little seaport at the foot of rocky Manhattan Island. The town was crowded far beyond the capacity of its inns and boarding houses, and all morning packet boats and stagecoaches brought visitors from the surrounding countryside. Everybody wanted to see George Washington. Many an aging citizen was heard to say that once he had laid eyes on "that noble face," he would be willing to die.

At dawn there was a salvo of cannon. At nine o'clock the church bells began. For half an hour they rang out merrily, welcoming the visitors. Then, after a pause, they began a solemn tolling, summoning the citizenry to prayer. By this time Washington, who had risen early, had dressed, had had his hair powdered and tied into a bag wig, had eaten his breakfast and read through the address on which he had been laboring for many weeks.

At ten o'clock, military units began forming at their barracks along Chambers Street, then almost at the northern limits of the city; and precisely at noon, a procession headed by the Congressional welcoming committee and made up of soldiers and bands arrived at Number 3 Cherry Street.

Before leaving the house, Washington folded the sheets on which his inaugural address was written, and stuffed them into the pocket of his long continental coat. His tastes in clothing ran to imported silks and satins, but for this event he had decided to advertise domestic industry. His simple dark brown suit came from a woolen mill in Hartford, Connecticut. Its plain metal buttons were embossed with eagles.

En route to Federal Hall, he rode alone in a carriage drawn by four horses. Ahead of him marched the Senatorial members of the Congressional committee, followed immediately by the troops. Behind him rode his secretary, the House members of the committee, Chancellor Livingston, and a few eminent citizens.

Starting at 12:30, the procession moved first in a more or less southwesterly direction along Cherry, a short lane now lost among the abutments of Brooklyn Bridge. Turning into Queen Street, it proceeded south to a point two blocks below Wall, where it bore right to follow Great Dock Street (now a part of Pearl Street) into Broad Street, so as to approach Federal Hall from the south. Two hundred yards short of the Hall, the troops broke ranks and formed a line on either side of the street. Alighting from his carriage attended by a small bodyguard, Washington walked through the avenue so made, while the crowds cheered.

Federal Hall had benefited greatly from its remodeling. Tuscan in style, it boasted seven openings onto Wall and Nassau streets. Four massive pillars in the center of the Wall Street side supported heavy arches, above which rose the four Doric columns fronting the twelve-foot-deep balcony off the Senate chamber. Thirteen stars had been worked into the panel of the cornice, and over each window were thirteen arrows encircled by olive branches.

Washington entered the building by the Wall Street entrance, crossed a marble vestibule, and mounted one of the wide stairways to the second floor, where the members of both Houses of Congress awaited him in the big front room used by the Senate. At the door of the chamber he was met by Vice President Adams, who led him to the chair of the presiding officer, on a platform sheltered by a crimson canopy.

Adams made the formal introduction. Then, turning to Washington, he said, "Sir, the Senate and the House of Representatives of the United States are ready to attend you to take the oath required by the Constitution. . . ."

Washington replied, "I am ready to proceed."

He was then escorted by Adams and a small group of dignitaries to the balcony. There a small table had been set up, covered with red velvet and surmounted by a cushion on which the borrowed Bible had been placed. As Washington appeared, the crowd outside burst into cheers. For a second he stood at the balcony railing with his hand over his heart. Then, as the people quieted, he took up a position behind the little table.

Chancellor Livingston stood a short distance away, at Washington's right. Between them was Secretary Otis of the Senate. When Livingston advanced to the table, Otis held the Bible for Washington. When the oath-taking was completed, the Chancellor said quietly, "It is done." Then, turning to the railing, he shouted, "Long live George Washington, President of the United States!" From the people jammed into the streets below and at the windows and on the rooftops of the surrounding buildings came a hurricane of sound. Simultaneously, cannon roared at the Battery and from vessels in the harbor, the church bells rang out again, and the Stars-and-Stripes were run up from the roof of Federal Hall.

Back in the Senate chamber, Washington read his address to a breathlessly still audience. His hands shook as he shuffled the pages of the manuscript. Occasionally his words were indistinct, partly because his teeth were troubling him, partly because he was never at his best on the speaker's platform. The address contained little in the way of concrete suggestions for the conduct of the new government. It dealt mostly in abstract political principles.

Its central theme was sounded in a single sentence: "The preservation of the sacred fire of liberty and the destiny of the republican model of government are . . . staked on the experiment entrusted to the hands of the American people."

When he finished, there was generous applause. Afterward several members of the audience walked with him to St. Paul's Chapel—nearby Trinity Church was closed for repairs—to attend a prayer service conducted by Bishop Provost.

All afternoon the people celebrated—in the shadow of the fort on the Battery, in the little park adjoining what was known as the "tea-water pump" in midtown, on the commons that stretched northward into the open country above Chambers Street. And in the evening there were fireworks.

☆ ☆ ☆

A twentieth-century political scientist[1] has described the office of the President of the United States as "one of the few truly successful institutions created by men in their endless quest for the blessings of free government." And to the development of this remarkable institution few individuals have contributed more than its first occupant.

It is not only the country that changes during the administration of every President. The Presidency itself changes. In the hands of "caretaker" or "custodial" Presidents—those who do not provide the nation with much leadership—its dimensions shrink. In the hands of strong Presidents such as Thomas Jefferson and Abraham Lincoln, James K. Polk, Grover Cleveland, and the two Roosevelts, they expand.

Every President since Washington's day has had one great advantage—Washington himself. Every subsequent President, no matter how extensive his difficulties, has

[1] Clinton Rossiter, in *The American Presidency* (rev. Mentor Book edition, 1964), p. 13.

found himself on a well-trodden path. To Washington fell the task of creating the path, of establishing principles that the Presidents who came after him could use as guidelines in coping with the problems of their times.

The verdict of history is that he did his job well. Without Washington, the Presidency would not be what it is today. In fact, it might not *be* at all.

One of Washington's problems arose from the mixed emotions with which the American people regarded their new government. For generations, every American had looked upon his colony, his state, as the political entity meriting his highest loyalty. In his youth Thomas Jefferson rarely spoke of Virginia as a state. He called it his "country." He stood ready at any moment to drink a toast to the King of England and to express his respect for the mother country, but in his heart Virginia came first.

Reluctantly, as the Revolution became inevitable, the thirteen sovereign states joined together to battle for their independence. Eventually they went a step further. They set up under the Article of Confederation a national government of sorts. This organization, the first American Confederacy, was little more than a league of states. It derived what few powers it had from the states, whereas the federal government that succeeded it derived its power directly from the people, irrespective of where they happened to reside.

When in 1787 the Constitution was submitted for ratification by conventions set up by the states, there ensued a debate as stormy as any that has taken place since, save for the one that engendered the Civil War. Only after long and agonized thought and much changing of minds was the

Constitution adopted. Even after it was put into effect, many Americans found it difficult to realize that they were now citizens of a nation first and of a state second. At this point, the new government had the support of their minds. One of Washington's jobs was to persuade them to give it the support of their hearts.

Numerous incidents showing how he worked to this end could be offered. One occurred in the fall of 1789, when the President concluded a tour of New England in Boston, where he reviewed a parade in his honor and then settled down for a brief visit. Chief man of Boston in those days was doughty John Hancock, he who in affixing his signature to the Declaration of Independence had proclaimed that he was writing it large enough for King George III to read without spectacles.

As Governor of Massachusetts, Hancock was of the opinion that no individual held an office more exalted than his own. On learning that Washington was in town, he sent a messenger inviting him to dinner at the Governor's house, adding that "due to a fit of the gout" he could not possibly call on the President.

One can imagine the frown gathering in Washington's gray eyes as he perused this note, muttering "*pretended* gout!" to himself as he did so. His reply to Hancock was austere. The President of the United States, it said, would be happy to receive the Governor of Massachusetts at his—the President's—lodgings.

Hancock got the point. Swathed in bandages, for his gout was not "pretended," he called on Washington. Ever since, it has been a fixture of American protocol that the President need not visit lesser officials. They must visit him.

A modern-day American President, Harry Truman, has headed the list of what he believes to have been America's six greatest decisions with the action taken by Washington in the Whisky Rebellion of 1794. This episode was the first major test of the President's powers. It grew out of the efforts of Washington's Secretary of the Treasury, Alexander Hamilton, to put the new government on a firm financial basis. During the Revolutionary War, both the nation and the states had piled up large debts. With Washington's blessing, Hamilton had got from Congress a law under which the general government not only undertook to pay its own debts in sound money but also agreed to assume—that is, to take over and pay—the remaining debts of the states.

Hamilton's "funding and assumption" policy, as it was called, was not universally popular. Critics said it favored the rich at the expense of the poor. Even some supporters were shocked on learning that it had enabled speculators in financial paper to line their pockets with money they did not deserve. In retrospect, the defects of Hamilton's fiscal devices seem small in contrast to their benefits. Both at home and abroad, they provided the United States with the good credit rating without which no government can survive.

To pay its debts, the general government had to levy a number of taxes. It was an excise tax on distilled spirits that touched off the troubles in the counties west of the Allegheny Mountains. The principal crop in these areas was corn. The farmers could get their product across the mountains to the Eastern markets most cheaply by shipping it in the form of whiskey. The "four-pence-a-gallon" tax cut their profits, and in October of 1794 the farmers in the

Monongahela Valley of western Pennsylvania announced they would not pay it and rose in armed rebellion.

It was a tense moment for Washington. Could he use force to compel the citizens of a sovereign state to obey a law passed by Congress? He decided that he could, and he did. Fifteen thousand federal troops were sent into the area. The rebellion was put down, and the taxes were collected. In afteryears many a harassed President, confronted with acts of disobedience in far-flung sections of the country, would be thankful for Washington's firm action in 1794.

By many such actions—some small, as in Governor Hancock's Boston; some weighty, as in the Monongahela Valley—Washington breathed life into the presidential office.

During his administration, the first major executive departments, including those whose chiefs sit in the Cabinet, were organized. The judiciary system, crowned by the Supreme Court, was established. The first ten amendments, the Bill of Rights, were added to the Constitution. A hundred and one governmental procedures, now taken for granted, were launched.

Although Washington made his own decisions, he consulted frequently with the members of his Cabinet. Often he consulted with them when there was no real need to. In doing so, he established a valuable precedent. Where most executive decisions are concerned, the chief magistrate is not required to consult with anyone; but nearly every President, taking a leaf from the first one, has made it a practice to seek advice regularly from the major functionaries of his department.

Unquestionably, Washington could have been elected

for a third term. By choosing not to run, he gave birth to a two-term tradition that continued unbroken until the days of Franklin D. Roosevelt. Now, of course, the two-term tradition is embodied in the Constitution. The twenty-second amendment, ratified February 26, 1951, makes two terms the maximum and bars the election for more than one term of a person who has held the Presidency for more than two years of a term to which some other person was elected.

In his famous Farewell Address, first published on September 19, 1796, but never orally delivered, Washington had words of advice. Where our relations with other nations were concerned, he urged Americans to maintain the position of neutrality formulated during his administration. Incidentally, the phrase "entangling alliances," often attributed to Washington's Farewell Address, was actually used by Jefferson in his first inaugural. What Washington said was that the United States should steer clear of *permanent* alliances with foreign nations and trust to "temporary alliances for extraordinary emergencies."

Washington also urged Americans to avoid what he called "factionalism," the division of the people into political parties. This advice, however, was doomed from the start. It did not conform with the realities of American life. The economic needs and political attitudes of the people were too varied. Governmental policies pleasing to the industrialists of New England were often displeasing to the corn growers of the Monongahela Valley and the tobacco planters of Virginia. Unless America was to be subjected to an endless series of revolutions, these divergent groups had to have men who could act as spokesmen for their views.

They needed political parties through which they could make their wants felt in the legislative halls of the general government.

The members of the political faction headed by Washington were called Federalists, a term coined to designate the supporters of the Constitution during the debate over its ratification. The tenets of Federalism were devised principally by Alexander Hamilton and John Adams. They envisaged an increasingly stronger central government, a gradual erosion of the power and influence of the states, and a body of legislation favorable to those citizens John Adams described as "the rich, the well-born and the able."

Throughout Washington's two terms, the voices of Americans at odds with the conservative attitudes of the Federalists grew steadily stronger. In the election of 1796, John Adams barely squeaked into the Presidency with an electoral majority of three votes. Under the Constitution as it then stood, the candidate who received the second highest number of votes automatically became Vice President, irrespective of his political inclinations. Politically, Adams's administration was divided, for his Vice President, Thomas Jefferson, was regarded as the major spokesman of the swiftly developing opposition group, the Republican or Democratic-Republican Party.

On balance, the second President's conduct of his office was admirable. A quarrel with France, begun under Washington, grew worse during Adams's administration. When clamors for drastic action arose all over the country, Adams sacrificed his chances for re-election by resisting them. With consummate diplomatic skill, he succeeded in averting what for a new and militarily unprepared country could have been a disastrous war. Unfortunately for the reputation of the second President, in the midst of these tensions Congress passed and he signed the disgraceful Alien and Sedition Acts.

Especially reprehensible was the Sedition Act. Scheduled to remain in force throughout the rest of Adams's term, it had the effect of making published criticism of the federal government illegal. Under its patently unconstitutional provisions, a score of newspaper editors were arrested and jailed. In the election of 1800 an outraged citizenry hurried to the polls to vote for the candidates of the new Democratic-Republican Party. Out went John Adams and with him, as a national influence, the Federalist Party.

The country had turned a corner. The Founding Fathers had created a Constitution. Now the people had created a device to make the Constitution work—the two-party system. Henceforth, in addition to the many duties imposed on him by law, every President of the United States would be obliged to serve as the chief of the political group that had put him in office.

Simultaneously, the nation was plunged into its first internal crisis—a battle in the House of Representatives that came close to bringing the new government to a tragically premature end.

3

"We are all Republicans, we are all Federalists"

☆ ☆ ☆

THOMAS JEFFERSON

On March 12, 1791, the *Weekly Ledger* of Georgetown, the busy shipping center on the Potomac River, announced that "Major Longfont, a French gentleman employed by the President of the United States," had arrived "to survey the lands contiguous to Georgetown where the Grand Columbian Federal City is to be built."

The Major referred to was Pierre Charles L'Enfant, the young architect who had designed and supervised the remodeling of Federal Hall in New York City. On his drawing board, L'Enfant drew up the plans for an urban wonderland reminiscent of Versailles, last capital of the Bourbon kings of his native France. The American capital was to have parks and circles, splendid buildings and broad and sweeping boulevards. Only a start was made on L'Enfant's ambitious plans. For lack of funds, they were soon placed in suspension. Almost a hundred years would pass before in 1889 the development of Washington, D.C., more or less in accord with L'Enfant's concepts, would be resumed.

When in 1800, during the closing months of John Adams's administration, the federal government moved from Philadelphia to its permanent home, the new capital was anything but grand. The houses of its three thousand inhabitants—109 of them of brick, the rest of frame—occupied scattered clearings in the woods or clung to the low hills along the eastern outskirts.

In startling contrast to the prevailing wildness, two unfinished buildings of impressive size rose above the trees. From the swampy banks of the river at the western end, the one later known as the White House lifted its sandstone walls. On the eighty-eight-foot hill a mile and a half to the west stood most of the relatively small section of the National Capitol that now serves as a link between the great circular room in the center and the extension sheltering the chamber of the Senate on the north.

A broad gash hacked through the wilderness between Executive Mansion and the Capitol was known officially as Pennsylvania Avenue, popularly as "the great Serbonian bog." The narrow wagon lane that meandered down the center of it was a continuation of the highway coming in from Georgetown to the west. Its roadbed was pitted with potholes and filled with tree stumps. In rainy weather, yellow mud buried the wooden walk flanking in on one side. In the adjoining marshes and wood lots, citizens hunted for snipe and fished in the sluggish waters of Goose Creek, a fair-sized stream that Thomas Jefferson was about to dignify by renaming it the River Tiber.

Eventually the original Capitol would consist of two legislative wings joined by a domed rotunda, but only the northern wing was standing on February 11, 1801, when the Houses of Congress assembled in joint session to count and open the electoral ballots cast during the recent national election.

Outside, a snowstorm raged. In the handsome new Senate chamber with its crowded galleries and gilded pillars, tension mounted as the anticipated results were announced. Federalist Adams had sixty-five of the electoral votes, and Federalist Charles Cotesworth Pinckney of South Carolina had sixty-four. The two Democratic-Republican candidates, Jefferson and Aaron Burr of New York, had seventy-three apiece.

In the case of a tie between the leading candidates, the Constitution then dictated that the House of Representatives must determine which was to become President, which Vice President. Accordingly, the Representatives retired to begin balloting.

Since their wing of the Capitol had not yet been erected, the House members were meeting on the west side of the building in the space now used by the Senate disbursing office. For six days beginning on Wednesday, February 11, the discomforts of these cramped quarters were aggravated by explosive oratory and fraying tempers. To become President, one of the two candidates must receive the votes of a majority of the states, nine in all. But ballot after ballot, the results remained the same: eight states for Jefferson, six for Burr, two divided.

A nagging question arose among the American people. What if inauguration day, less than a month off, came and went and no President was chosen? It was reported that if the deadlock were still unbroken by March 4, the defeated Federalists would hold on to the Presidency by force. Alarmed by these rumors, two Democratic-Republican governors served notice that they stood ready to send their militia to Washington in the event of an effort by the opposition to usurp the government. By the weekend it was plain that, unless a decision were reached soon, the country faced civil war.

The House was still dominated by the Federalists. In a tumultuous party caucus held as the balloting began these gentlemen decided to support Burr. Their reasoning was that the clever New York corporation attorney would be more sympathetic to their economic interests than the gentleman-farmer from Virginia. The crisis was resolved by behind-the-scene maneuvers in which one of the major figures was Federalist James A. Bayard, the lone Representative of the little state of Delaware.

Not until some years later did Bayard reveal the general nature of these maneuvers. Even then, the versions given by other participants were sufficiently contradictory to place their exact nature in the realm of historical mystery. Bayard said that Jefferson assured the Federalists that, if elected, he would not disturb some of their more cherished policies. Jefferson admitted making most of the statements attributed to him, but said they were simply an expression of his intentions; they were not promises offered to secure the election.

As for that curious man, Aaron Burr—his conduct was so honorable that Bayard concluded that he was not the scoundrel some people thought him to be, but a fool. According to the Delaware Congressman, Burr could have snatched the Presidency with ease simply by playing a little politics. Burr did nothing of the sort. Instead, in letters to associates, he made clear his realization that it was the will of the American people that Jefferson be elected to the Presidency.

It *was* their will, and on the thirty-sixth ballot the House bowed to it. Jefferson was elected by the votes of ten states, and Burr became Vice President. The country heaved a sigh of relief, and to avoid another tie vote in the electoral college, Congress proposed, and the states ratified, the twelfth amendment to the Constitution. Under this, the electors now vote separately for President and Vice President.

☆ ☆ ☆

In the late hours of the night of March 3, 1801, President John Adams was busy at his White House desk. Scorched on one side by a roaring fire on the hearth, chilled on the other by the March winds seeping through the leaky walls of the unfinished mansion, he was signing the appointments of numerous Federalists to government offices in a last-minute effort to save the country from the chaos he foresaw following the inauguration of his successor on the next day. At midnight he gave the container holding his blotting sand a final shake and called for his carriage. Leaving his lively minded wife Abigail to attend to the details of moving, he had himself driven out of town.

Washington had attended Adams's inauguration, but Adams had no intention of attending Jefferson's. As his great-grandson Henry Adams would later reveal, the last Federalist President was convinced that the "second American Revolution" was at hand. He felt that for him to be present at the installation of a Democratic-Republican would be as inappropriate as for King George III to have appeared at the installation of President Washington. Alone with his gloomy thoughts, he was well on his way to Baltimore when at daybreak the rattle of artillery broke the silence of Washington and ushered in the first inaugural ceremonies to be held in the permanent capital.

☆ ☆ ☆

The swearing-in proceedings, the delivery of the inaugural address, and what the local newspaper, *The National Intelligencer and Washington Advertiser*, called "a pretty general illumination" in the evening—these were the highlights of Wednesday, March 4, 1801. Jefferson's first inauguration was marked by greater simplicity than that of any other regularly elected President. In part, the lack of pageantry reflected the gifted Virginian's natural indifference to such things. In part, it reflected his respect for the value of symbolism. In holding the ceremonies to a minimum, he notified the country that a new and more democratic era had begun.

Jefferson and John Adams had once been close friends, and the current political chill between them would thaw in the near future. As the Sage of Quincy and the Sage of Monticello, respectively, they engaged in a long and lively correspondence. Jefferson's name was among the last words spoken by John Adams when on Independence Day, 1826, death came to him in Massachusetts, only a few hours after the death of Jefferson in Virginia. The two men shared a trait and a conviction. Both were large-minded. Both believed in the rule of the *aristoi,* in government by the best people. On this issue their only difference lay in their ideas of who was best. Adams was inclined to think of the best as limited to the wealthy and the well-born. Jefferson was certain that hidden away in every backwoods hamlet were men who, with sufficient education, could as capably run the government as any Harvard-trained aristocrat on Boston's Beacon Hill.

Since the transfer of the general government to Washington, Jefferson had been living at Conrad and McMunn's boarding house on a stretch of land overlooking the grounds of the new Capitol. A rambling frame structure surrounded by livery stables, Conrad and McMunn's stood on the site now occupied by the $8 million First House Office Building Annex on the southwest corner of New Jersey and Independence avenues.

Space was at a premium in primitive Washington. The governmental factotum who found himself in a room with only one other occupant was lucky. As Vice President, Jefferson had a room to himself. He was also given the exclusive use of a private parlor on the first floor. He asked and received no other privileges. Although at fifty-seven he was the oldest resident of the house, his place in the dining room was a seat toward the lower end of the long common table.

On inauguration morning—a day of chill but pleasant weather—one of his first callers was Samuel Smith, editor of *The National Intelligencer.* To Smith the President-elect handed a copy of his inaugural address. When a few hours later the people left the Capitol after the swearing-in ceremonies, the newsboys were hawking the first inauguration extra, a printed copy of the speech Jefferson had just delivered.

About ten o'clock a company of riflemen and one of artillery, both from Alexandria, appeared on New Jersey Avenue and paraded back and forth in front of the President-elect's lodgings. At noon Jefferson came out, a tall, spare man with loose sandy hair, a lean and freckled face, a gentle mouth, and keen gray eyes. He had not purchased a special outfit. Both his knee-length brown suit and his red waistcoat had seen considerable wear.

Accompanied by a few friends and followed by the Alexandria militia units, he made his way among the tree stumps and across the broken land of the clearing to the Capitol a hundred paces to the north. He entered the building under a discharge of artillery.

Awaiting him in the Senate chamber, according to *The National Intelligencer*, was "the largest concourse of citizens ever assembled in Washington"—about three hundred, including the two Houses of Congress, the Justices of the Supreme Court, and a scattering of ladies. All rose as the President-elect stepped in. Vice President Burr, who had already taken his oath, escorted him to the chair of the presiding officer. Jefferson seated himself there, with Burr on his right and the young and recently appointed Chief Justice of the United States, John Marshall, on his left. Then, after a second of silence, he rose and began reading his address.

The National Intelligencer found his manner "plain, dignified . . . unostentatious" and "chatte," but it is doubtful if everybody in the chamber heard him. Like Washington, Jefferson was not at home on the speaking platform. There were no oratorical flourishes. His voice was weak. But if the delivery of the address was not impressive, the contents of it were. Included were several of the thoughts that have rung across the years to become imbedded in the fabric of American life—thoughts that must have come as a shock to listeners who had lived through the election campaign that had started him on his way to office.

The presidential election has the same effect on the American people that the full moon is said to have on dogs. They go a little mad. Emotion and exaggeration take over. Reasonable men accept as sanctified fact statements that in an off-election year they would dismiss as feverish fancies. In this respect, the campaign of 1800, the first to be based on a two-party system, had given the country a foretaste of things to come.

Even though John Adams had split with Hamilton and now headed what Jefferson's followers considered the less obnoxious wing of the Federalist Party, they still feared that, if re-elected, Adams would continue Hamilton's "moneyed system"—a financial system they regarded as beneficial only to the rich. They considered Adams a monarchist at heart. They took the recent marriage of his son,

John Quincy Adams, to the daughter of an English-born woman as proof that the President had united "his house to that of His Majesty of Britain," with the idea of making John Quincy the first "king of America."

The thought of Jefferson in Adams's chair filled all Federalists with horror. In Europe, the French Revolution had run its erratic course. Napoleon had seized power. France and England were once again on the verge of war. Jefferson's known sympathies with the French revolutionists prompted the Federalists to charge that if elected he would weaken the American Army and Navy, "under the guise of economy." Then, by a show of friendship to France, he would involve the United States in a hopeless war with England. One of their most virulently repeated charges was that the Virginian was an atheist who would destroy the churches. Jefferson was on record as a states-rightist, a believer with Tom Paine that the best government is the least government. The Federalists charged that as President he would so dismantle the powers of the general government that it would once again become the feeble thing it had been under the Articles of Confederation.

It was against this background of charge and countercharge that Jefferson delivered his first inaugural. Speech experts say that the form in which he cast it set a pattern that has been followed by four fifths of his successors. More to the point, he laid the groundwork for a practice that has seen the country through some of its most trying moments —the willingness of the rival political parties, in times of high emergency, to cooperate.

The spirit of bipartisanship breathed from his words as he reminded his audience that the political wars were over for the time being. The man who now stood before them represented, not a faction, but the whole people.

"Every difference of opinion," he said, "is not a difference of principle. We have called by different names brethren of the same principle. We are all Republicans, we are all Federalists. If there be any among us who would wish to dissolve this Union or to change its republican form, let them stand undisturbed as monuments of the safety with which error of opinion may be tolerated where reason is left free to combat it."

When he had finished, he turned to his left, and John Marshall, rising, faced the first of the five Presidents he would, as Chief Justice, swear into office. Then, having taken the oath, Jefferson walked back to his boarding house to eat lunch, sitting in his usual place at the lower end of the long dining-room table.

☆ ☆ ☆

Even some of Thomas Jefferson's most sympathetic biographers have echoed the charge made by his enemies in his own day that his eight-year administration was a tissue of inconsistencies. They point out that in the election campaign of 1800 he went before the country as a believer in limited central government, but that after becoming President he went to the other extreme. They argue that he "out-federalized the Federalists," using the powers of his office with such vigor that when he left the White House in 1809 the general government was stronger than it had ever been.

Their résumé of what happened during his administration is accurate. But the charge of inconsistency can be accepted only with reservations. Its origin dates back to the great quarrel between Jefferson and Hamilton in the days when both sat at President Washington's Cabinet table. In a political quarrel, extreme views on one side tend to beget extreme views on the other. So Jefferson, in an effort to combat Hamilton's extremely conservative schemes, sometimes countered with extremely radical ones of his own.

For a time Hamilton had his way, but by 1800 the political outlook of the country had changed. Hamilton's ideas were losing ground. When Jefferson became President, there was no longer any need for him to endorse extreme propositions. Hence the tone of his first inaugural. That conciliatory address was an announcement that as President he intended to occupy what politicians call a moderate or middle-of-the-road position.

It has been said that no man ever gets to the White House without surrendering or altering some of his principles. In fairness to Jefferson, we can say that there is no evidence that he abandoned or altered any of his principles *before* getting to the White House. Some alterations took place after he arrived there, but in every case they were dictated, not by a desire to get something for himself, but by the wish to benefit his country.

Throughout his adult life, Jefferson was an American first and a political philosopher second. Like George Washington and John Adams, he looked on the great experiment in self-government as unique, one that must not be allowed to fail. Long before becoming President, he had urged the youth of the Republic to get their education at home. He feared that if they went to Europe for it, they might absorb ideas and traits "alarming to me as an American."

There were people who read into the Declaration of Independence, as written by Jefferson, a call for and a justification of perpetual revolution. Jefferson saw it otherwise. He said the Declaration was merely "an expression of the American mind" intended "to place before mankind the common sense of the subject." The phrase "common sense" was often on his lips. On another occasion he said, "I can never fear that things will go far wrong where common sense has fair play."

Common sense and his country's welfare—these concepts represented his basic and guiding principles, and with these concepts his presidential actions were as consistent as he knew how to make them. Right or wrong, every important decision of his administration took what he believed to be the common-sense approach to the problem and was made on the assumption that he was doing what was best for America.

☆ ☆ ☆

The most memorable accomplishment of Jefferson's administration was an outgrowth of developments on two continents. One was the increasing importance of the Mississippi River to the farmers of the American West. The other was the emergence of Napoleon as the dictator of France and the scourge of Europe.

When Jefferson became President, the western boundary of the United States lay along the Mississippi from Canada to the northern limits of what is now the state of Louisiana. On the far shore of the river lay the Louisiana Territory, a vast area stretching for unmeasured distances into the West.

Originally the territory, including its capital city of New

Orleans, was a French possession, but since 1762 it had belonged to Spain. In 1800, ownership changed again. Under a treaty, kept secret for a year and a half, the territory and its capital were returned to France.

The revelation that New Orleans was now in the hands of Napoleon was alarming to Jefferson. The livelihood of thousands of Western Americans depended on the Mississippi, or, more exactly, on their being able to ship the products of their farms through the port of New Orleans, near the mouth of the river.

Under a treaty with Spain, the Americans had duty-free access to New Orleans. The prospect that Spain might some day suspend this right (as for a while she did) was not a source of too much worry. Trouble with weak Spain could be handled. Trouble with powerful France presented a more formidable problem. One possibility was especially disturbing to the President. In the event of trouble with France, the United States might have to seek the protection of France's enemy, England. That would throw America into the sort of alliance with a European nation that Jefferson, and Washington before him, had warned against.

Jefferson acted promptly. He sent a diplomatic mission to Napoleon with instructions to seek some arrangement under which Americans would be guaranteed permanent access to New Orleans.

The results of this mission far exceeded his expectations. At this point in his spectacular career, Napoleon was looking hard into the future. He had abandoned previous plans to send soldiers to New Orleans by way of extending his empire into the New World. The growing might of England on the sea told him that such an undertaking could not work. His determination now was to concentrate instead on his plans for bringing all of continental Europe under French influence.

Convinced that in the near future England would take New Orleans from him by force, he decided to get what he could out of it by selling the city to the Americans. To make the proposition more attractive, he threw in the entire Louisiana Territory.

At first Jefferson hesitated. Acceptance of Napoleon's startling offer would involve him in a step contrary to his often-expressed views concerning the limitations of presidential power. One of his chief quarrels with the Federalists arose from their differing opinions on how the Constitution should be interpreted. The Federalists endorsed the doctrine of implied powers. According to this doctrine, the President, in performing the duties imposed on him by the Constitution, could take whatever actions were necessary, even though the Constitution did not give him, in so many words, the right to take such actions. Jefferson contended that the President could do only what the Constitution expressly said he could, and the Constitution did not expressly empower him to add to the territory of the United States.

He considered asking Congress to propose, and the states to ratify, an appropriate amendment, but he discarded this idea when he realized that time was of the essence. It would take months to put through an amendment. Meanwhile Napoleon might withdraw his offer. In the interests of thousands of hard-working farmers on the frontier, he ordered his diplomats to conclude the treaties necessary for the transfer of the Louisiana Territory. With the ratification of these documents by the Senate on October 21, 1803, the size of the United States was more than doubled.

☆ ☆ ☆

Less successful were Jefferson's efforts to cope with a problem generated by the Napoleonic Wars.

This long and complex military development began with the French dictator's futile attempt to invade England in 1803. It ended with his final defeat at Waterloo, in Belgium, in 1815. In the early years of the conflict, Napoleon swiftly increased his dominion over the lands of continental Europe. During the same period, England seized dominion over the oceans.

To American shipowners, the war in Europe was a boon. France could no longer send ships to pick up rum and sugar in the productive French West Indies, but America could. Then in 1805 England announced that she would no longer permit American vessels to carry French cargoes. English warships began patrolling the Atlantic sea lanes. American privateers were intercepted, boarded, and searched. Some were seized, and thousands of sailors were forced to leave their American vessels to serve in the British Navy. England's excuse for this exasperating behavior was that the majority of these sailors had been born in America when it was an English colony. "Once an Englishman," roared the seagoing lion, "always an Englishman!"

Throughout the United States, large numbers of people shortly to be known as the Warhawks began calling on the President and Congress to declare war on England. Aware that the country was militarily unprepared, Jefferson resisted these clamors. On July 2, 1807, he issued an embargo proclamation designed to placate the Warhawks and to bring pressure on the British to desist from their violations of the freedom of the seas.

The embargo closed American ports to English ships and kept American ships at home. It pleased the Warhawks, but it distressed the commercial interests of New England. Despite the harassment of American vessels by the British, the New England shipping trade was still lucrative. As the embargo took effect, New England seaports fell idle. Her textile mills, dependent on overseas markets, closed down.

The embargo accomplished nothing, and after fifteen months, squeezed between the embittered New Englanders and the Warhawks, Jefferson was compelled to lift it. It might have helped by giving the United States time in which to prepare for what was to be the War of 1812 if the President had seen fit to build up American defenses. But he neglected to do this. When he retired from office, the international situation was as precarious as ever, and under his successor, James Madison, the United States embarked on its second war with England.

It was still unprepared. There is no saying how the War of 1812 might have ended if England had not been too busy with her affairs in Europe to give her troubles in the New World proper attention. Fortunately for the struggling new Republic, a war that was a victory for nobody was followed by a peace that was definitely a victory for the United States.

The treaty of peace drawn up in 1814 did not so much as mention England's violations of the freedom of the seas. It did contain provisions advantageous to the American economy. Prosperity and political calm—the Era of Good Feeling—prevailed throughout the administration of Madison's successor, James Monroe.

Only in the West were there significant signs of discontent. Jefferson had said that there was "no safe depository of the ultimate powers of society but the people themselves." During the Era of Good Feeling the complaint along the frontier was that too much of the country's power was deposited with the commercial classes of the Northeast. The time had come for more of it to be placed in the calloused hands of the men who were clearing the forests and carrying American civilization into the valleys of the Ohio and Mississippi rivers.

Bent on exercising more control over their government, the frontiersmen looked about for a political organization to work for them and a spokesman around whom they could rally. The organization was created for them principally by such Eastern politicians as Aaron Burr and Martin Van Buren, who eventually deleted the word "Republican" from Jefferson's old Democratic-Republican Party to form the Democratic Party. The frontiersmen found their spokesman in hard-bitten "Old Hickory," General Andrew Jackson of Tennessee, veteran of the Indian Wars and hero of the Battle of New Orleans, greatest of the American victories in the War of 1812.

In the national election of 1824, Old Hickory received the highest popular vote of four leading candidates, but there was no majority in the electoral college. Again the selection of a President was consigned to the House of Representatives, where political manipulation and plain luck awarded the prize to John Quincy Adams of Massachusetts.

During the second Adams's well-intentioned but ineffectual administration, the winds of democracy reached gale force. There were now twenty-four states. In 1824, six of them, including populous New York, were still permitting their legislatures to appoint the presidential electors. In 1828, the legislatures had this privilege only in South Carolina and Delaware. In all of the other states the people went to the polls, and in November, Andrew Jackson was swept into the Presidency with fifty-six percent of the popular vote.

A few months later his followers began converging on Washington, prepared to let the world know that the common people of America had come into their own by making inauguration day, March 4, 1829, the wildest celebration of freedom the country has ever seen.

4
The breeze from the West

☆ ☆ ☆

ANDREW JACKSON

To hear Andrew Jackson say "I do solemnly swear . . ." people came to Washington from points as much as five hundred miles away, then an uncomfortable journey of several days. During the fortnight preceding the inauguration, over ten thousand people poured into the little capital. There were backwoodsmen and fur trappers, log-cabin farmers and Indian fighters, "blab-school" teachers, and the keepers of "groceries," as the frontier saloons were called. A contemporary observer described them as men who "spat accurately, swore eloquently and sang loudly the praises of Old Hickory."

Their unpolished ways, their picturesque languages, and their coonskin caps and buckskin jackets did not make a favorable impression on the more respectable residents of the Federal City. An associate justice of the Supreme Court sniffed that the "Reign of King Mob" was about to begin. Senator Daniel Webster of New Hampshire felt a "breeze from the West" and sadly concluded it was an ill wind. Approached with a request to escort the President-elect to the Capitol to take his oath, the only uniformed light infantry company in the District of Columbia haughtily refused. The scandalized leaders of the local elite likened the democratic invasion to the sack of ancient Rome by the Barbarians.

Time was to prove their fears exaggerated. And a look through their windows would have assured them that Washington was not yet Rome.

The Federal City had grown since Jefferson's day. The population now totaled close to thirty thousand. Its still mostly wooden structures occupied 1,150 city blocks. Pennsylvania Avenue had assumed its present width, 160 feet, and had been covered with macadam. This change, along with some other stretches of macadam or cobblestone, gave the city fifteen miles of paved road.

Downtown Washington, along the northern side of the avenue between the Capitol and the White House, boasted several moderately comfortable hotels, the shop of a portrait painter, a theater, and a school where young ladies could study orthography, plain and ornamental needlework, and "astronomy (with the use of the globe)."

The National Capitol stood complete as originally planned. The park surrounding it, although less extensive than now, had been graded and partly landscaped, and enclosed by an iron picket fence. Save for the still unfinished East Room, the White House also stood as originally planned. Six hundred and fifty gallons of white paint hid the black scars left on its walls by the invading British during the War of 1812. A scattering of red brick buildings had been erected to house the federal departments, and *The National Intelligencer* spoke proudly of the city's three public markets, its "neat" infirmary and "splendid-looking" jail.

Notwithstanding these improvements, Washington was still almost as ramshackle and slattern as any town of comparable size on the frontier from which so many of the supporters of the "People's Candidate" had come to see him inducted into office in 1829.

☆ ☆ ☆

At sixty-two, Andrew Jackson retained the tall lean erect figure of his youth, the long and narrow face with its burning blue eyes. Only the stiff hair, striking up from his high forehead like a wing, had lost its youthful look, the once reddish-brown having given way to the gray of age. Born on the North Carolina border shortly after his father's death in 1767, and left on his own by the death of his mother fourteen years later, Jackson had come to his present eminence along odd byways and curious detours.

His twenty-first year found him in the infant town of Nashville in the Western Range, the section of North Carolina soon to be Tennessee. Here he set out to become a frontier gentleman by diligently cultivating the best people and by speculating in land. As a lawyer and later as a jurist, he consistently sided with the creditor class known as the "Beaver Hats" against the hard-pressed debtor class, or "Beaver Skinners," who regarded him as one of the loftier local "nabobs." As one of his biographers has written, the man destined to be the People's Candidate "was ever an aristocrat at heart."

Prior to his acquisition of the tract of land where his mansion "The Hermitage" still stands in Nashville, Jackson lodged in the home of the widow of Colonel John Donelson, wealthy land speculator and one of the founders of the Tennessee capital. Also resident in the home was the Donelson's beguiling daughter Rachel, who had separated from her unstable husband, Lewis Robards. In 1791 Rachel's friendship with Jackson prompted her to petition the state legislature for a divorce. Later that year, Rachel and Jackson were married, unaware that the divorce action was not yet complete. Although a second wedding ceremony was performed when the divorce became final, gossip continued to accuse Jackson and his wife of having lived in sin.

As a thirteen-year-old boy serving with the American Revolutionary forces, Jackson had acquired a taste for military exploits. Not until the outbreak of the War of 1812 was he given another chance to indulge it. Then, as Major-General of the Tennessee militia, an elective office, he helped subdue the hostile Creek Indians in the Battle of Horseshoe Bend on March 27, 1814. His success at the Bend won him a commission as Major-General in the Army of the United States. It was in this capacity, on January 8, 1815, that he commanded the forces that saved New Orleans from three attempts by the British to seize it. The subsequent news that the peace treaty had been in effect for two weeks at the time of the battle did nothing to diminish Jackson's status as the greatest American hero of the conflict.

After New Orleans, he was a marked man. A group of New York and Tennessee politicians began erecting the political machine that came close to putting him into the Presidency in 1824 and landed him there in 1828.

For Jackson, victory was shadowed by personal tragedy. A month and a half before the inauguration, his wife died. Their marriage had been a love match, and their affection had been deep. It was a somber and subdued man who on February 11, 1829, left the Hermitage to begin his triumphal journey to Washington.

En route to the Federal City, the President-elect and his party enjoyed a leisurely trip by steamboat down the Cumberland River and up the Ohio. From Pittsburgh they traveled by land, reaching Washington on February 17. At first, all of the presidential party put up at the Indian Queen (subsequently the Metropolitan), one of the Pennsylvania Avenue hotels. Later the President-elect moved to Gadsby's Hotel at Sixth Street. There, judging from the prices posted by the other avenue hostelries, his daily expenses ran to about $1.25 for board and room, plus another dollar for such extras as candles and a fire on the hearth.

It was the custom for the incoming President to call on the man whose chair he was about to assume, but Jackson could not bring himself to take this step. Years of affluence had given the General the manners of a gentleman, but behind his courtliness lurked an explosive temper that had involved him in several duels and in at least one bloody tavern brawl. Less than a decade earlier, his harsh treatment of Indian tribes placed under his jurisdiction had made him the subject of investigations in Washington. On two occasions he was saved from national disgrace by the intervention of John Quincy Adams, then serving President Monroe as Secretary of State.

Jackson's emotions knew no halfway point. He either loved or hated, and his gratitude to the man who was now President did not survive the violent election campaign of 1828, in which he and Adams were the leading opponents. Newspapers friendly to the President published slanders about Mrs. Jackson—slanders that to the end of his life her husband regarded as having hastened the death of his Rachel. When President Adams made no effort to halt these ugly attacks, the General's affection for him soured. On his part, Adams, brilliant but touchy, was hurt by Jackson's failure to call on him. When inauguration day arrived, he followed in the footsteps of his father, becoming the second President to absent himself from the induction of his successor.

☆ ☆ ☆

On inauguration day the weather, according to *The National Intelligencer*, was serene and mild. The crowds were out early. Hundreds of people were already on their way up the hill to the plaza in front of the east portico of the Capitol when at dawn the cannon barked at the Navy Yard. By midmorning the streets were a milling mass of noisy citizens. Daniel Webster found the spectacle depressing. "I never saw such a crowd here before," he observed, "and they really seem to think that the country has been rescued from some violent danger." A Washington attorney named Francis Scott Key, who sixteen years before had written a rousing anthem entitled "The Defense of Fort McHenry, or the Star-Spangled Banner," found the people "beautiful" and their enthusiasm "sublime."

At 10 a.m. the police and other peace officers of Washington and Georgetown assembled in the chamber of the Supreme Court to receive instructions from the District Marshal. According to a lukewarm acount of the day in *The National Intelligencer*, an Adams newspaper, the Marshal offered some advice for handling the "brigade of pickpockets" who had descended on the city and whose "depredations to date" indicated that the common people of the frontier were by no means poverty-stricken. Two voluntary marshals, a Colonal Hunter and a Dr. Carson, were dispatched to Gadsby's Hotel to escort the President-elect.

At 11 a.m. a group of survivors of the Revolutionary War, organized the day before and already known as the Immortals of Washington, marched to Gadsby's, where their leader, Colonel William Polk of North Carolina, delivered a congratulatory address to the President-elect. Then, bareheaded and dressed in a plain black suit without an overcoat, the old general began the six-block walk up Capitol Hill, accompanied by the Immortals and the two voluntary marshals.

By this time, approximately twenty thousand people had gathered in front of the east portico. The excited rumble of their voices reached to the foot of the hill. Coming abreast of the picket fence surrounding the Capitol grounds, the Hero of New Orleans paused for a brief conference with his companions. Then, with a boost from the voluntary marshals, he vaulted the fence, walked across the grounds, and entered the building by the western door, unspotted by the throng impatiently awaiting his arrival on the other side.

At 11:30 a.m. he entered the Senate chamber. There, John Caldwell Calhoun of South Carolina, who had served as Vice President under John Quincy Adams and had been reelected to the same position under Jackson, had been sworn in half an hour before.

Although some governmental dignitaries had not yet arrived, the fan-shaped chamber was already crowded. In the western gallery sat the members of the House of Representatives. In the eastern gallery the frock coats of Washington gentlemen mingled with the linsey-woolsey of the frontier. A large number of ladies were among the visitors seated to the rear of the Senators' chairs and in the lobby beneath the eastern gallery.

One observing Washingtonian noted that as Jackson marched "down the aisle with a quick, large step, as though he proposed to storm the Capitol," he was wearing two pairs of spectacles. This was the General's practice. One pair was for reading, the other for seeing at a distance. The pair not in use lay across his head. "On this occasion," reported the eyewitness being quoted, "the pair on his head reflected the light; and some of the rural admirers of the old hero were firmly persuaded that they were two plates of metal let into his head to close up holes made by British bullets at New Orleans."

On the platform the President-elect seated himself in a chair immediately in front of the Senate secretary's desk. A few minutes later Chief Justice Marshall and the other members of the Supreme Court came in and took the seats assigned to them on the right of Jackson's chair. Already occupying the seats to his left were the brilliantly uniformed foreign ministers and their suites.

At noon the Senate was adjourned, and a procession was formed to escort Jackson to the balcony of the then stepless east portico. At the appearance of the President-elect the throng went wild. There was a surge in the direction of the balcony. The General would have been mobbed had it not been for the foresight of the District Marshal. That official had supplied his policemen with a length of ship's cable. This steel barrier, hastily put in position, kept the crowd at bay.

Like Jefferson, the General spoke first and then took his oath. The contents of his address were unspectacular, his delivery stiff. When he finished repeating the oath, salutes were fired by two companies of artillery stationed in the vicinity of the Capitol.

A white charger had been brought to carry him to the White House. The Immortals provided him with a seemly bodyguard, but the raggle-taggle of people following him down Pennsylvania Avenue scarcely amounted to a parade. No line of march, no effort by one citizen to keep step with another; only a formless moving mass of cheering celebrants.

The approach to the White House had all the earmarks of an attack on that sedate residence. The crowd flowed across the lawn and into the house itself. Frightened servants, alarmed lest the furnishings be destroyed, closed and locked the doors. A futile precaution. Those still outside promptly made for the windows and continued to push in. Within the stately rooms, draperies were ripped down. Chairs were smashed. Sofas were muddied by the boots of citizens unable to make progress across the crowded floors.

Everybody wanted to shake hands with the new President. Jackson had faced the Indians at Horsehoe Bend, the British at New Orleans. But this onslaught by his admirers was too much. Pressed against a wall of the East Room, he took advantage of an open window to escape. Once outside, he retreated across the city to the relative safety of Gadsby's Hotel.

Behind him, the roistering continued. The appearance of tubs of orange punch brought a stampede, with servants thrown to the floor and trampled by thirsty guests. Further damage to the house was averted when the surviving attendants managed to empty it by carrying the tubs out to the lawn.

From the lawn the revelry spilled over into the rest of the city. All afternoon the taverns did a roaring business, supplying the merrymakers with sherry cobblers and gin slings, mint juleps, timber doodle, snakeroot bitters, and eggnog. In the evening some went to the inaugural ball at Carusi's, some to the theater to witness a performance of "the elegant comedy *The Belle's Stratagem,*" preceded by a "Jackson Overture" composed by the orchestra leader. A few gathered at the better restaurants to climax an exhausting day with generous portions of beef smothered in onions, mutton, ham, pheasant, turkey, ice cream, jelly, and fruit.

☆ ☆ ☆

To the Presidency, Jackson brought neither a fully developed program nor much political experience. He had served his state in Congress three times, once as a Representative, twice as a Senator. He had completed neither of his senatorial terms, and his record in both Houses was devoid of distinction. In the politics of his own Tennessee, his only action of consequence had been to support the moneyed classes in an argument over the establishment of a state bank.

In spite of this thin and essentially conservative political background, his conduct as President more than lived up to the expectations of his followers. Loyalty to those who were loyal to him was one of the more attractive traits of this aggressive, quarrelsome, resourceful, self-reliant, and appealing man. When after eight stormy years in the White House he returned to his Hermitage in Nashville, he was one of the few Presidents to leave office more popular than when he came in.

Some historians still question the degree to which his presidential actions actually benefited his followers. Concerning his intentions, however, there is little or no argument. Just as every decision of Jefferson's administration was made in what the great Virginian believed to be the best interests of the country as a whole, so every decision of Jackson's administration was made in what he believed to be the best interests of the farmers and planters in the West and South, and of the workers in America's growing cities.

So far as the future was concerned, what Jackson did was probably not so important as the atmosphere he created. The policies he followed had the effect of encouraging Americans to make a more strenuous effort than before to realize the still far from completely attained ideal expressed in the assertion of the Declaration of Independence that "all men are created equal."

One of the more significant events of his administration was set in motion in 1828 when Congress passed, and the

President reluctantly signed, what some people called the "tariff of abominations."

Since Washington's day, the tariff had been a source of friction among Americans. In New England and in most of the other Northern states, people made their living primarily by the manufacture and sale of goods. These people wanted the federal government to require foreign manufacturers to pay a high duty on whatever goods they shipped into this country. They favored a "protective tariff"—high enough to protect American industries against competition from outside the country. Such protection enabled American industrialists to charge more for the products of their factories.

In other parts of the country, and especially in the South, a high tariff was not popular. Southerners preferred "a tariff for revenue only"—just big enough to help the federal government meet its debts and keep its financial house in order. Directly or indirectly, most Southerners made their living by selling cotton and tobacco to Europe. Since they had few industries of their own, they had to buy whatever manufactured goods they needed. Naturally they were always happiest when foreign competition forced the domestic industries from whom these purchases were made to lower their prices.

No sooner was the "abominable" tariff passed than cries of outrage arose throughout the South. State legislatures sent memorials to Congress, protesting that the tariff was unfair; if left on the books, it would impoverish Dixie. Shuddering over the terrible word even as they uttered it, people began talking about "nullification": the deliberate refusal by a state to obey a law of the United States. The

Senate became the scene of a celebrated debate—Robert Y. Hayne of South Carolina versus Daniel Webster, with Hayne arguing that when a federal law proved harmful to one of the states, it had a *right* to nullify it.

It was known that Southern-born Jackson disapproved of the abominable tariff. But what view did he take toward the Southern contention that a state had a right to ignore a federal law?

The answer came on April 13, 1830, when the Democratic governors of the country gathered in Washington for a Jefferson birthday rally at the Indian Queen Hotel. After the dinner there were toasts. Governor after governor arose to proclaim his sympathy with the right to nullification. The President was the last to rise, glass in hand. The few words of his toast went clanging across the land:

"Our Union: It must be preserved!"

Deeds were soon added to words. Two years later, one of the Southern states, South Carolina, formally announced its intention of ignoring the federal tariff laws within its own borders. Jackson countered with a proclamation calling the South Carolina action a treasonable attempt to dissolve the Union by violence. Simultaneously he sent warships to the harbor of Charleston with a warning that the import duties required by the United States laws would be collected at that South Carolina port by force if necessary. Meanwhile, under the supervision of Henry Clay, a compromise tariff schedule, more satisfactory to the South, was arranged. Placated by the compromise, South Carolina bowed to the President's commands.

So the nullification crisis came, and so it passed. We know now, of course, that it was only a curtain-raiser to the more intense controversy that twenty-nine years later terminated in the Civil War.

Responsible for this controversy was a combination of social and economic developments that is so much a part of our collective memory as Americans that it calls for only brief review. Negro slavery, always at the heart of the dispute, was older than the Republic. It had taken root on American soil in the early years of the colonial era.

Many of the Founding Fathers, when they assembled in Philadelphia in 1787, were eager to see a ban on slavery in the Constitution. Unhappily, efforts to insert such a ban were resisted by some of the Southern representatives. These delegates argued that the big cotton and tobacco and sugar plantations on which the economy of their states depended could not be operated without slave labor. To keep the "more perfect Union" from falling apart before it could be put together, a clause was placed in the Constitution saying, in effect, that slavery could be retained by those states that had no objections to it.

Before the end of Jefferson's first term in the White House, the sectional pattern of the future had been set. North of what is roughly the thirty-ninth parallel on the map of America—the Mason-Dixon line—lay the free states and territories, where human bondage was forbidden by law. South of it lay the slave states.

The features of the Northern culture were commercial enterprise, small farms, and free labor. The culture of the South was dominated by the great plantations, where most of the work was done by human beings whose owners regarded them as property.

What was good for the North was not necessarily good for the South. Consequently, a struggle for power took shape. All went well as long as the number of free and slave states could be kept about even, giving each section about the same amount of influence in Washington. But this became difficult as the country grew, eventually to occupy the entire lower half of North America from Atlantic to Pacific. Beginning in the 1830's, it was made even more difficult by the rise of the anti-slavery movement in the North. There, as time moved on, more and more citizens opposed the extension of slavery into the territories. They demanded that slavery be kept out of all future states, that it be confined to those states where it already existed.

In the beginning, few Southern leaders believed their "peculiar institution," as slavery was known in Dixie, to be morally right. They were content to defend it as a necessary evil. But as the anti-slavery movement spread throughout the North, their attitude changed. What some historians call the New South emerged. Its spokesmen argued that slavery was a positive good. Some insisted that the "peculiar institution" was divinely ordained. By 1850, what had been an economic and political issue had become a moral issue. Economic and political differences can often be resolved by compromise. Moral differences are not so easily settled.

From the backwoods of Illinois in the winter of 1860 came a tall and melancholy-looking man to deliver a political address at Cooper Union in New York City. Fifty-one-year-old Abraham Lincoln had served his county in the Illinois legislature and his state in the United States House of Representatives. Recently he had made an unsuccessful bid for the United States Senate. In the course of this election campaign he had attracted considerable attention by engaging in a series of debates on the slavery question with Senator Stephen Arnold Douglas, Illinois's feisty "Little Giant."

Although a heavy snow was falling on the night of the speech—February 27—fifteen hundred people showed up, filling Cooper Union auditorium with the largest "representation of the intellect and culture of our city" since the days of Clay and Webster, according to Horace Greeley's New York *Tribune.*

It was no ordinary event. Lincoln was a prominent member of the Republican Party recently organized by the antislavery elements of the North. He was being mentioned as a possible presidential candidate in the forthcoming national election. In the opinion of his supporters, he suffered only one serious handicap. He was not well known in the East. Naturally their eyes were on Cooper Union that snowy evening; and naturally the rapt attention with which Lincoln was listened to encouraged them, as did the delirious applause for his words. Leaders of the slave-state South were watching too; but what they saw, or more precisely what they heard, did not please them.

Not that Lincoln was an abolitionist. He respected tradition, he revered the Constitution. He did not believe that the federal government had the right to interfere with slavery in those states where it already existed. As for its extension into the territories, that, in his opinion, Congress had the power to forbid and should forbid.

Talk was running through the country that if the Republicans won in November some of the Southern states would secede from the Union. Lincoln called on the members of his party to prevent this by making it clear that the Republicans had no intention of interfering with slavery in the present slave states. Would the Southern leaders believe such an assurance? Lincoln doubted it. His guess was that the South would not trust the North until the North admitted the rightfulness of slavery as an institution.

"All they ask," he said of the Southern spokesmen, "we could readily grant, if we thought slavery right; all we ask, they could as readily grant, if they thought it wrong. Their thinking it right, and our thinking it wrong, is the precise fact upon which depends the whole controversy. Thinking it right, as they do, they are not to blame for desiring its full recognition, as being right; but thinking it wrong, as we do, can we yield to them? Can we cast our votes with their view, and against our own? In view of our moral, social, and political responsibilities, can we do this?

"If our sense of duty forbids this, then let us stand by our duty fearlessly and effectively. . . . *Let us have faith that right makes might, and in that faith let us, to the end, dare to do our duty as we understand it.*"

When a few months later Abraham Lincoln was elected President of the United States, South Carolina seceded from the Union. Six other Southern states quickly did the same. When on February 11, 1861, the President-elect left Springfield, Illinois, to journey to Washington to be sworn in, the seven seceded states had drawn up their own constitution and established on a provisional basis their own independent government, the Confederate States of America.

In huge black type, a South Carolina newspaper described the greatest crisis the unique American experiment in free government had faced. THE UNION—said this headline—IS DISSOLVED!!!

5
"The great and durable question"

☆ ☆ ☆

ABRAHAM LINCOLN

On the evening of February 21, 1861, almost a hundred thousand people poured into the narrow lanes of downtown Philadelphia and into the lobby and parlors of the Continental Hotel on Chestnut Street to pay their respects to Abraham Lincoln.

The President-elect had arrived late that afternoon, en route to Washington from his Illinois home. Ten days before, standing on the rear platform of his train, he had bidden goodbye to his Springfield neighbors. At that time he gave voice movingly to his affection for the town he was leaving and to his seemingly abiding fear that he would never return to it alive.

All along the line, wherever his train stopped, in big cities or at tiny railroad settlements, crowds gathered to look on his towering frame and scraggly face, to wring his hand and cheer him on. Everywhere, in response to the demands of the people, he delivered brief and mostly impromptu speeches.

None of them was marked by the eloquence of the Cooper Union speech that had won him so many Eastern votes in the November election. Profoundly disturbed by the rebellion in the South, he was unwilling to reveal his plans for coping with it until he possessed the presidential powers to do so. All along the line he was hard put to speak without saying anything and to disguise his own inner alarm with an air of optimism and confidence.

So dense were the crowds in downtown Philadelphia following his arrival there that two grim-faced men, moving toward the Continental Hotel about 9 p.m., had to squeeze and claw their way to its gaslit entrance. The younger of the two, a small, bearded man with the burr of his native Scotland still in his voice, was Allan Pinkerton, founder of one of America's first private detective agencies. His companion was Norman Buel Judd of Illinois, one of Lincoln's campaign managers—a short, chunky man with a broad and ruddy face, a hooked nose, and a flowing white beard.

As one of Lincoln's traveling companions, Judd, like the President-elect, had taken quarters at the Continental. Then, having work to do and wishing to escape the crowds, he had rented another and quieter room at the St. Louis Hotel a few blocks away. It was to his room at the St. Louis that Pinkerton had come, accompanied by Samuel M. Felton, president of the Philadelphia, Wilmington and Baltimore Railroad. A consultation among the three men ended with the decision by Pinkerton and Judd to hasten to the Continental for a talk with Lincoln.

It took them an hour to cover the short distance. By the time they reached the Continental, Lincoln had left the reception line in the parlor and retired to his suite. Judd and Pinkerton, apprised of this fact, got a message to the President-elect, requesting him to join them. A few minutes later Lincoln, Judd and Pinkerton were engaged in earnest conversation in Judd's quarters.

Lincoln's published plans called for him to raise an American flag early the next morning at Independence Hall in honor of Washington's birthday. Following this ceremony, he was to travel to Harrisburg to address a joint meeting of the Pennsylvania legislature. From there he was to move on to Baltimore. To make his connections in Baltimore, he was to travel by carriage from the point of his arrival, the Calvert Street Station, to the Baltimore and Ohio Station, a one-mile drive across the Maryland city.

What sort of reception awaited him in Baltimore was not known. A delegation from every large community he was to visit to date had joined him well in advance to escort him into town. But so far no group from Baltimore had made arrangements to do this, and it was known that the city was filled with Southern sympathizers.

According to Pinkerton, a group of these sympathizers were planning to assassinate Lincoln as he passed through Baltimore. The information gathered by Pinkerton operatives indicated that the conspirators might lose their nerve at the last minute. All the same, the detective's advice to the President-elect was to take no chances. He urged Lincoln to leave Philadelphia that night, using a train that would permit him to pass through Baltimore well in advance of his scheduled arrival there.

Lincoln did not turn down this suggestion in its entirety. He pointed out that he had promised to take part in the flag-raising ceremonies at Independence Hall on the following morning. He had also promised to speak to the legislature in Harrisburg in the afternoon. He was determined to keep those commitments. Once he had finished his Harrisburg speech, however, he was ready to follow whatever course Pinkerton thought best.

What the President-elect did not reveal until much later was that shortly after his talk with Pinkerton he received a message sent from Washington by Senator William H. Seward of New York, who was to be his Secretary of State. Seward, too, had heard of a plot to kill the President-elect in Baltimore. The New Yorker's information, coming from a source completely independent of Pinkerton and his operatives and supplemented later by the same information from a third independent source, convinced Lincoln that an attempt might be made on his life if he clung to his travel plans.

At six o'clock the next morning he was at Independence Hall in Philadelphia. On the previous January 29, Kansas had been admitted to the Union. The flag raised by the President-elect that morning was the first to carry a star representing the new state. It displayed thirty-four stars in all.

Apparently Pinkerton's words were on Lincoln's mind as the flag was unfurled. In a brief speech to the crowd gathered for the ceremony in the pale morning light, he mentioned the statement in the Declaration of Independence that "all men are created equal." Then: "If this country cannot be saved without giving up that principle," he said, ". . . I would rather be assassinated on this spot than surrender it. . . . I have said nothing but what I am willing to live by, and if it be the pleasure of Almighty God, to die by."

After his speech in Harrisburg in the afternoon, he was invited to dine and spend the night at the home of the Governor of Pennsylvania. He declined on the grounds that he was not feeling well. Then, hastening to his hotel, he began making the preparations that would get him to Baltimore in the middle of the night.

In Philadelphia, competing manufacturers had presented him with two tall beaver hats. Friends who asked Lincoln which of the hats he considered the better were treated to an example of his tact and humor. "They mutually surpass one another," he told them. The donor of one of the beavers had placed in the same box a soft felt hat of a type Lincoln never wore. In his room at the Jones House, his Harrisburg hotel, he donned an old overcoat and stuffed this soft hat into his pocket.

His reason for choosing it, he explained later, was that people were accustomed to seeing him in a tall beaver. In the slouch hat, which he put on as he slipped from the hotel by a back door, "I was a different man."

In accordance with the plans made by Pinkerton and Judd, he traveled to West Philadelphia on a special train consisting of one passenger and one baggage car. Every precaution was taken to keep his movements a secret. As the special train left Harrisburg at about six in the evening, the telegraph lines linking that city to Baltimore were cut.

In West Philadelphia, reached shortly before ten that evening, reservations awaited him on the sleeping car routed to Washington by way of Baltimore. They had been obtained by one of Pinkerton's operators, a Mrs. Kate Warne. She had purchased them in the names of her "invalid brother" and a companion.

Traveling with Lincoln were Pinkerton and Ward Hill Lamon of Illinois, one of the President-elect's former law partners. Lamon was of a melodramatic turn of mind. At one point he attempted to impose on Lincoln a bowie knife, a pistol, and a derringer. Lincoln waved this armory aside, and Pinkerton scolded at the rough and ready Illinois frontiersman. "If any fighting is necessary, Mr. Lamon," he said, "you and I will do it."

The Calvert Street Station in Baltimore was reached shortly before 3:30 in the morning. At this point the car bearing the President-elect was drawn across the city to the Baltimore and Ohio Station. It had been chosen for this reason. So accustomed were the local citizens to the passage of the Washington sleeping car at this hour that they paid no attention to it. As the horse-drawn railroad carriage bumped and rattled its way through the silent streets, Lincoln smiled to himself as out on the back platform another passenger suddenly broke into the stirring verses of "Dixie."

At six o'clock in the morning, February 23, the sleeping car arrived at the old Washington railroad station at Second and Pennsylvania avenues on what is now part of the Mall. Waiting to carry Lincoln to the Willard's Hotel in his carriage was Congressman Elihu Washburne of Illinois.

☆ ☆ ☆

On the eve of the inauguration the most deeply troubled man in Washington was General Winfield Scott, commanding general of the armies. At seventy-five, "Old Fuss and Feathers," as he was known, was a bloated caricature of the dapper young General Scott who in 1814 had led the American troops to victory over the British in the Battle of Lundy's Lane, and of the already elderly but still handsomely proportioned General-in-Chief Scott who in 1848 had defeated the Mexicans.

Ordinarily, only militia were used to accompany the incoming President to the Capitol and back, but disturbed by continuing rumors of assassination plots, General Scott averred his intention of guarding Lincoln with regular army men. The infirmities of age added vigor to his grumbles when the Congressional committee on arrangements pointed out that in largely pro-secessionist Washington the appearance of regular soldiers in the inaugural parade might provoke the very incidents the General was trying to avoid. Irascibly, reluctantly, he agreed to a different plan, under which his regular soldiers would proceed, unbeknown to the parade spectators, along streets parallel with the parade route.

In addition, he posted riflemen on the roofs of the buildings overlooking Pennsylvania Avenue. "Watch the windows on the opposite side," were his orders, "and fire on them in case any attempt should be made to fire on the presidential carriage." Like the soldiers relegated to the side streets, the riflemen were to keep out of sight. Ostensibly Lincoln would be protected only by members of the District militia, with a squadron of cavalry from Georgetown and a company of West Point cadets thrown in to give dash and color to the procession.

Numbering a population of 61,122, the Washington of 1861 was twice as large as Andrew Jackson's Washington. Even so, the visitors swarming into town for the great day overtaxed its facilities. People slept six to a room in the hotels. Some spent the night in the hallways of commercial buildings or in the areaways of the new marble Patent Office Building at Seventh and F streets Northwest. In preparation for the parade, the now cobblestoned roadbed of Pennsylvania Avenue was scraped of accumulated grime. When inauguration day dawned, chill and damp under a cloudy sky, the parade route from the White House to Capitol Hill lay between two unsightly mounds of brown dirt.

The outgoing President, handsome James Buchanan of Pennsylvania, spent the morning at the Capitol signing bills passed at the last minute by the outgoing Congress. During the preceding decade, the present House and Senate extensions had been added to the Capitol, at the urging of the man who was now President of the Southern Confederacy, former Senator Jefferson Davis of Mississippi. At its points of greatest dimension, the marble and sandstone building now extended 350 feet from east to west, 751 feet and 4 inches from north to south. Its hauntingly beautiful façades enclosed three and a half acres of legislative halls, offices, committee and reception rooms, dining areas, kitchens, crypts, corridors, bars, rotundas, and entrance foyers.

In 1855 the wooden dome over the central rotunda had been removed. The present 9-million-pound cast-iron dome was halfway up, with steel derricks gaping skyward above its unfinished slopes. In the grass fringing the plaza in front of the east portico of the Capitol, the plaster model of the 19½ foot statue of Armed Freedom, destined for the apex of the new dome, reposed in a litter of marble blocks.

At noon Buchanan left the Capitol and returned to the White House. Thence, accompanied by a Senate committee, he went to Willard's Hotel to pick up Mr. Lincoln. Holding to a moderate pace, the presidential party proceeded in open carriages along the avenue, surrounded by the military and followed by thousands of citizens in carriages, on horseback, and on foot.

At the Capitol the presidential party entered the building over a temporary wooden ramp leading to the northern entrance. Meanwhile, in the Senate, Lincoln's Vice President, Hannibal Hamlin of Maine, had been sworn in. The members of Congress, the Justices of the Supreme Court, the foreign ministers and their aides, the press corps, and the elite of Washington society had taken their assigned places under the eagle-embossed skylight of the new red-and-gold chamber.

Immediately after the entrance of the presidential party, a procession was formed and Lincoln was escorted to the east portico. Here, in accordance with long custom, a wooden platform had been erected above the steps and painted off-white to match the huge building behind it. It consisted of three sections, a covered center and two open wings. To conserve space, chairs had been placed only in the center. Most of the people privileged to occupy the presidential platform stood throughout the ceremonies. Nevertheless, the business of arranging them properly consumed the better part of an hour. Among those seated with the President-elect were Mrs. Lincoln and Illinois's "Little Giant," Senator Douglas, who had been Lincoln's chief rival in the presidential election.

So brilliantly has the light of research been turned on this high moment in American history that its details have been blurred. Legend and fact have become all but hopelessly intertwined. Some contemporary accounts say that as Lincoln approached the little table on the platform to give his address, the cheers of the ten thousand people below him reverberated beyond anything ever heard on the premises before. Others say the heckling of pro-Southern groups in the crowd easily exceeded the enthusiasm. As Lincoln rose, he removed his tall silk hat, only to discover that there was no place to put it. Senator Douglas kindly relieved him of it. This may or may not have happened, but Douglas is reported to have said later, "Well, if I can't be President, at least I can hold the President's hat."

One New York newspaper reported that as Lincoln reached the little table the clouds parted above and a shaft of sun, unseasonably warm for March, fell about the scene. Another New York newspaper reported that at this moment a dust storm roared in from the West, caused presumably by a sudden gust of wind picking up the debris stacked along Pennsylvania Avenue.

Lincoln was presented to the crowd by his close friend from Oregon, Senator Edward D. Baker. "Fellow citizens," Baker said, "I introduce to you, Abraham Lincoln, the President-elect of the United States."

As Baker retired, Lincoln laid his manuscript on the little table and pulled a pair of steel-bowed spectacles from his pocket. This action was a signal for merriment in a portion of the crowd. A lusty, hawk-eyed fellow cried out, "Take off them spectacles, we want to see your eyes." Another man remarked loudly, "I didn't know he wore glasses, they ain't in the picture." At about the same time a small man with fiery red whiskers began making a little speech of his own, only to be shushed up rapidly by the disgusted people around him. Soon after Lincoln began, a small boy who had found a seat in one of the trees tumbled to the ground. Apparently he was uninjured. The record ends with his plop into the grass and what a reporter described as a "quick look of sympathy" from the tall man on the platform.

Nearly all reporters agree that Lincoln spoke in a clear, firm voice that was heard by most of his listeners. He was nervous at first. In this relatively elegant world to which fate had assigned him, he was often conscious of his Western mannerisms, of the nasal twang in his high voice, of his seeming inability to find a suit of broadcloth that would hang properly from his gaunt figure.

Framed in the Capitol doorway behind him, as he spoke, was Senator Louis T. Wigfall of Texas, one of the leaders of the Southern secession movement. According to Lincoln's poet biographer, Carl Sandburg, the contempt and defiance in Wigfall's eyes expressed "in pantomime" what he had been saying in the Senate—that the old United States was now a corpse. The only remaining question was how "to give it a decent burial." All over the country, in Sandburg's paraphrase, thirty million people were asking, "Mr. Lincoln, since you can't coax the seceded states back, will you go so far as to use force and start a bloody civil war?" In the opinion of the fire-eating Senator from Texas, Abraham Lincoln did not have "the backbone" to do that.

It is a pity no one thought to make note of whatever changes of expression came over Wigfall's broad features as the President-elect spoke on. Much of the address was indeed conciliatory, an attempt to woo the rebelling states back by making it clear that the government-to-be had no intention of disturbing their peculiar institution. But as Lincoln came to the high points of his remarks, it became plain that he stood ready to do whatever was necessary to keep the republic intact.

"I hold that in contemplation of universal law and of the Constitution," he said, "the Union of these States is perpetual. . . . It follows . . . that no State upon its own mere motion can lawfully get out of the Union; that *resolves* and *ordinances* to that effect are legally void, and that acts of violence within any State or States against the authority of the United States are insurrectionary or revolutionary, according to circumstances. . . . The Union . . . *will* constitutionally defend and maintain itself. . . . The power confided to me will be used to hold, occupy, and possess the property and places belonging to the Government and to collect the duties and imposts. . . . The mails . . . will continue. . . . A husband and wife may be divorced and go out of the presence and beyond the reach of each other, but the different parts of our country can not do this. They can not but remain face to face, and intercourse, either amicable or hostile, must continue between them. Is it possible, then, to make that intercourse more advantageous or more satisfactory *after* separation than *before?* Can allies make treaties easier than friends can make laws?"

His closing words, like his opening ones, were directed to the people of the South:

"In *your* hands, my dissatisfied fellow-countrymen, and not in *mine*, is the momentous issue of civil war. . . . We are not enemies, but friends. We must not be enemies. Though passion may have strained, it must not break our bonds of affection. The mystic chords of memory, stretching from every battlefield and patriot grave to every living heart and hearthstone all over this broad land, will yet swell the chorus of the Union, when again touched, as surely they will be, by the better angels of our nature."

When the address was finished, Lincoln was sworn in by eighty-one-year-old Chief Justice Roger B. Taney, participating in his ninth and last presidential inauguration. Then came the big parade down the avenue, a luncheon at Willard's Hotel, a reception at the White House, a ball and other festivities in the evening.

As Lincoln made ready to spend his first night in the White House, the words of his address were going by telegraph as far as St. Joseph, Missouri. From that point, pony-express relays rushed them west. Before they could reach Sacramento, California—seven days and seventeen hours later—Lincoln was struggling with the problem of what to do about a small federal garrison cooped up behind the walls of Fort Sumter in the harbor of Charleston, South Carolina, within range of Confederate guns on nearby islands and shore. Not quite a month later, on the morning of April 12, the booming of these guns signaled the beginning of one of the saddest and bloodiest conflicts of all time.

☆ ☆ ☆

During the opening years of the Civil War, the major objective of the North was to preserve the Union. As time moved on, the abolition of slavery became a secondary objective. On January 1, 1863, Lincoln issued his Emancipation Proclamation. The Civil War President was always careful to designate this document a war measure, primarily intended to demoralize the enemy.

The Proclamation did not abolish slavery. It did not free any slaves. Its provisions applied only to the ten Confederate states over which the Union at that time had no control. Specifically exempted from its provisions was the eleventh Confederate state, Tennessee, because much of that state was then occupied by federal troops under a military governor appointed by Lincoln. Nor did the Proclamation apply to the four slave-holding border states—Delaware, Maryland, Kentucky, and Missouri—who had chosen to fight on the side of the Union. The abolition of slavery did not take place until December 18, 1865, with the ratification of the thirteenth amendment to the Constitution.

Lincoln lived just long enough to see the war come to a virtual end with the surrender by Confederate General Robert E. Lee to Union General Grant at Appomattox Courthouse, Virginia, on April 9, 1865. Six days later America's greatest President was dead, the victim of an assassin.

☆ ☆ ☆

Every war is followed by a period of reconstruction, but it is the twelve troubled years after Lincoln's death that Americans have in mind when they speak of *the* Reconstruction.

No stretch of American history has proved more difficult

to understand. What went wrong and why—we are still struggling with these questions in our continuing effort to find out where we came from so as to understand better where we seem to be going.

Before the Civil War, Lincoln had spoken of the dispute over the right or wrong of slavery as "the great and durable question." That question was disposed of on the battlefields. Slavery vanished, to be replaced after the war by another great and durable question: How were four million freedmen, the men and women and children who had been slaves prior to the war, to be incorporated into American society? How were they to climb from slavery to full-fledged citizenship?

It was a long journey for ex-slaves. Almost none was educated. Almost none had any political experience. The onetime slaves were not even in a position to make a start for themselves. That had to be done for them either by the states or by the federal government.

Lincoln's successor was his second-term Vice President, Andrew Johnson of Tennessee. A Southerner and an oldfashioned states'-rights Jacksonian Democrat, Johnson wanted the states to handle the problem. His chief Republican opponents in Congress, known as the Radicals, objected. The Radicals and their followers wanted the federal government to handle it. They argued that to put the control of the Southern Negro into the hands of the former Confederate states was to put him at the mercy of his former masters. Around this issue, complicated by many others, a quarrel of epic proportions broke out between the stubborn President and the Radical-dominated Congress.

Congress won. Over a series of presidential vetoes, the

Radicals pushed through a series of Reconstruction Laws. These laws had two immediate effects. They filled the South with federal soldiers and they compelled the one-time Confederate states to set up Republican governments acceptable to the Radicals. The result was what is known as Radical Reconstruction, a brief period marked by unrest and violence and corruption in government throughout the South.

Unquestionably much of this turmoil was simply the natural aftermath of a terrible war. Just as unquestionably, much of it was either caused or aggravated by Radical Reconstruction. In any event, some historians, looking back upon these unhappy times, have concluded that the Reconstruction as a whole was a "tragic era" and an "age of hate."

Tragedy there was. Hate there was. But the period was not all darkness and the Radicals were not all evil. Many of them were sincere in their desire to help the Negro obtain his civil rights. To this end, they succeeded in adding two significant amendments to the Constitution—the fourteenth and the fifteenth.

Among other things, the fourteenth amendment installed the Negro as an American citizen and directed the states to give him the same legal protection they gave to their white citizens. The fifteenth amendment forbade the states to deny the vote to any citizen because of his race. In the generations that followed, many states found ways of getting around the clear intent of these directives. Nevertheless, the amendments remained in the Constitution, a source of hope and strength to the Negroes in their struggle for equality.

A judicious judgment on the Tragic Era comes from the

pen of Kenneth M. Stampp, a twentieth-century student of the period. "The Fourteenth and Fifteenth Amendments, which could have been adopted only under the conditions of radical reconstruction," Professor Stampp has written, "make the blunders of that era, tragic though they were, dwindle into insignificance. For if it was worth four years of civil war to save the Union, it was worth a few years of radical reconstruction to give the American Negro the ultimate promise of equal civil and political rights."

Radical Reconstruction did not last long. By 1876—the year of the "disputed election"—eight of the one-time Confederate states had shaken off their Radical-Republican governments and substituted Democratic regimes satisfactory to their white citizens. Only in three Southern states—Florida, Louisiana, and South Carolina—were the federal troops still on hand and the Radical Republicans still in control.

In the election of 1876 the presidential nominees were Republican Rutherford B. Hayes of Ohio and Democrat Samuel J. Tilden of New York. Tilden won the popular vote with a majority of 250,000, but trouble arose when the Republicans challenged the electoral-college figures from four states, including the three Southern states still under Radical dictation. An alarming deadlock ensued. To break it, Congress set up an electoral commission, empowered to decide whether the disputed electoral votes should go to Tilden or to Hayes.

By this time the leadership of the Radical wing of the Republican Party had changed drastically. Its more earnest pro-Negro adherents had either died or lost their influence in the group or simply left it in disgust at the miseries of Radical Reconstruction. The Radicals were now far more interested in putting their man in the White House than in helping the Southern Negro. A deal was arranged, under which the disputed electoral votes were given to Republican Hayes with the understanding that he would withdraw the federal troops from the South and restore home rule to all of the once Confederate states.

Whatever the details of the deal, that is exactly what happened. Hayes was elected, the troops were withdrawn, and complete home rule was restored. By these actions, Reconstruction was officially terminated. As for its unfinished business—the civil status of the Negro—that was put to one side, to be revived during the civil-rights movements of our own times.

☆ ☆ ☆

In drawing up the Constitution back in 1787, the Founding Fathers were guided by their conviction that only power can check power. With this in mind, they endeavored to impart to each of the three coordinate branches of the federal government, and especially to the legislative and executive branches, an approximately equal amount of strength.

For the first sixty-some years of our national life, from Washington to Lincoln, the Congress and the President were indeed about equal. Neither succeeded for any length of time in dominating the other. Throughout the Civil War, however, the Presidency moved to the foreground. This development did not occur because Abraham Lincoln desired it but because the awful struggle he was called upon to resolve made it imperative that he assume almost dictatorial powers.

After Lincoln's tragic death, the inevitable reaction set in. Congress took over and for the next thirty-two years, except during the divided terms of Cleveland, the Presidency assumed a position of secondary influence in national affairs.

Then in the summer of 1900 there took place one of those little accidents that so often alter the course of events. That summer an ebullient, bucktoothed, nearsighted young Republican named Theodore Roosevelt was completing his first term as Governor of the State of New York. Speaking softly but carrying a big stick, to quote one of his own never excessively modest descriptions of himself, Governor Roosevelt had initiated some reforms annoying to the big insurance companies of his state.

In those days the pre-eminent political figure in New York was the boss of the Republican Party in that state, bearded, thin-faced Thomas C. Platt. As was the case with all the political bosses of his era, Platt's major job was to keep the treasury of his party well filled by making sure the financial moguls of New York were ever in a happy frame of mind. When Governor Roosevelt offended the big insurance companies, he also offended Boss Platt.

Since Roosevelt was popular with the people, Platt was averse to attacking him openly. He was equally averse to letting T.R. have a second term as governor. To get him out of the state, he saw to it that he was kicked upstairs. As a result, when on March 4, 1901, McKinley began his second term as President, forty-two-year-old Teddy Roosevelt was his Vice President.

Political maneuver was supplemented by act of God. When only a few months after the opening of his second term McKinley was assassinated, Theodore Roosevelt became the youngest man ever to occupy the White House and the first of the strong modern Presidents.

6

"Let the thing be done"

☆ ☆ ☆

THEODORE ROOSEVELT

The robust and frequently smiling man who stepped onto the inauguration platform in Washington on March 4, 1905, was no stranger to the American people. Long before his elevation to the Presidency by the death of McKinley three and a half years earlier, Theodore Roosevelt had caught the public fancy—as a hard-working member of the Civil Service Commission under President Benjamin Harrison, as the corruption-hunting head of the New York City Police Board from 1895 to 1897, as Assistant Secretary of the Navy during McKinley's first term, and as a picturesque lieutenant-colonel charging up Cuba's San Juan Hill in 1898 with the First Regiment of U. S. Cavalry Volunteers, popularly known as the Rough Riders, in a decisive battle of the Spanish-American War.

Born into a prominent New York family of inherited mercantile wealth, Teddy had learned self-discipline in the school of illness. Asthma, defective vision, poor hearing, abscesses on thighs and legs—he had overcome these handicaps by vigorous exercise in the great outdoors. Never, however, was he merely an activist. His mind was as curious as his body was busy. He read voluminously and studied hard, and eventually earned a respected place for himself as a historian and a naturalist.

When he took over the Presidency on September 14, 1901, he was "dee-lighted" to discover that "the White House was a jolly pulpit." A citizenry accustomed to the comfortable platitudes of McKinley and the meatier but still narrowly political pronunciamentos of Cleveland found itself listening to a President determined to air his views on such wide-ranging subjects as simplified spelling, the novels of the French author Émile Zola, and the currently raging argument between the advocates of birth control and the proponents of "the full baby carriage."

Since Lincoln, all of Teddy's predecessors in the White House except Cleveland had operated under the principle that their primary domestic function was to execute the laws as passed by Congress. A President of this inclination —nineteenth-century McKinley and twentieth-century Coolidge are good examples—takes care to avoid any action that might be construed as encroaching on the prerogatives of the legislature or as interfering in the private sector of the economy.

This was not Teddy's way. Once he concluded that a situation demanded presidential initiative, he didn't care what he encroached on or with whom he interfered. President

Benjamin Harrison once described him as "a rather impatient sort." Roosevelt, Harrison said, "always wanted to put an end to all the troubles of the world between sunrise and sunset." Henry Pringle, whose biography of T.R. is one of the most absorbing done on any President, says that Teddy always believed the federal system to be a "government of men, and not of laws." His philosophy as President, to quote Pringle, was: "Let the thing be done, and worry about the law and the details afterwards."

Teddy's autocratic methods are demonstrated by an incident that took place soon after his assumption of his high office. By the turn of the century, America had become a world power. The people of America knew it, but T.R. wanted the world to know it too. So he decided to send the fleet around the world as a demonstration of American might.

As Commander-in-Chief, he had a perfect right to do this. What he didn't have was the necessary money. When the fleet left American shores, there was just enough money in the coffers of the Navy to get it about halfway around the globe. Congress grumbled, but T.R. was undisturbed. He reasoned that Congress would never permit the United States fleet to lie stranded at the other end of the earth. He was right. Once the departure of the fleet was presented to the country as an accomplished fact, Congress contented itself with a few more grumbles—and then appropriated the funds required to bring it back home.

Even more highhanded were the manipulations by which he obtained for his country control over the little section of Central America where the Panama Canal now carves its way. The need for a waterway linking the Atlantic and the

Pacific oceans had been a topic of conversation since the days of Andrew Jackson. Not until the turn of the century, however, were concrete steps taken to obtain the right to dig a canal through the Isthmus of Panama.

Since the little country of Panama belonged to neighboring Colombia, an arrangement was drawn up with that South American republic. Under the Hay-Herran Treaty, as the arrangement was known, the United States agreed to pay $10 million down and $250,000 annually after nine years in return for a perpetual lease on what is now the Canal Zone.

When the Colombian parliament refused to ratify the Hay-Herran Treaty, Roosevelt forced the issue. It was all done very deftly—and trickily. Panama was encouraged to revolt against Colombia, and an American warship was so placed in neighboring waters that Colombia could not possibly quell the rebellion. Panama became independent and set up a government which the United States promptly recognized. Then the United States concluded with Panama the treaty it had been unable to get from Colombia.

At the turn of the century, America's international position was an enviable one. She had indeed become a world power, and her citizens were reveling in all the advantages accruing to a nation in that exalted position. To Theodore Roosevelt goes the credit for being the first President to point out to the American people that world power also involved responsibilities beyond our shores.

As a result of the Spanish-American War, two one-time Spanish colonies had fallen within the orbit of United States influence. The island of Cuba, in the Caribbean, had become an independent nation more or less under American protection. The Philippines, far out in the Pacific, had become the wards of this country.

To insulate Cuba against European interference, T.R. inspired the first doctrine to be added to American foreign policy in almost a hundred years. Throughout the preceding century the cornerstones of American foreign policy had been the Proclamation of Neutrality issued by Washington in 1793 and the Monroe Doctrine issued by President Monroe in 1823. Washington's neutrality proclamation was aimed at preventing this country from becoming involved in the quarrels of Europe. Monroe's doctrine was aimed at preventing Europe from exercising control over the independent nations of Latin America, that is, Central America, South America, and the Caribbean.

T.R.'s addition to these basic principles was called the Roosevelt Corollary to the Monroe Doctrine. The Corollary said that since financial difficulties within a Latin American nation made it vulnerable to European intervention, the United States had the right to step in and assist any Latin American government unable to meet its financial obligations. Within the Western Hemisphere, in other words, this country had become an international policeman.

Words without deeds were not T.R.'s way. The Corollary was soon implemented. On one occasion, American troops were hustled down to the financially shaky Dominican Republic in the Caribbean. On another, the Marines were dispatched to Cuba. In addition, into the constitution of the new Cuban republic went an amendment framed by Senator Orville H. Platt of Connecticut. The Platt Amendment, destined to remain in effect until the days of Franklin Roosevelt, permitted the United States to intervene in the affairs of Cuba whenever the legitimate government there appeared to be in trouble.

To protect the Philippines against both European and Asian interference, T.R. engaged in a variety of diplomatic maneuvers that had the effect of extending American influence across the Pacific. One of these maneuvers, his settlement of the war between Russia and Japan in 1905, won him the Nobel Peace Prize.

A lion abroad, he was no lamb at home. In his handling of the country's domestic problems, he is best remembered as the great "trust-buster."

Before the Civil War, the United States was an Arcadia, a land of agrarians. After the Civil War came the Industrial Revolution. In what seems in retrospect but the twinkling of an eye, America was transformed from a land of farms and plantations and small towns into a land of factories and cities. In 1860, only a little more than a billion dollars were invested in American manufacturing and the country had only half a million industrial wage earners. By the time Teddy Roosevelt acceded to the Presidency in 1901, capital investment in manufacturing had risen to more than $12 billion, and the number of industrial wage earners to five and a half million.

This sweeping change brought the country great material benefits—and new problems. People pouring into the cities to work in the factories created the slum as we know it today. Once, the majority of Americans had owned land and had derived the bulk of their income from it. Now the majority of them had only their wages and salaries. When these were good, the country boomed. When they weren't, there was depression and financial panic. The country was beset with ills unknown to pre-Civil War America, with periods of mass unemployment and bread lines, with strikes and other forms of industrial strife.

In 1879 a group of oil producers combined to form the Standard Oil Trust. In rapid succession, other large industrial combinations were set up to control lead, beef, sugar, linseed oil, and whiskey. All over the country, people began talking ominously about "monopolies." Not only did the trusts force innumerable small businessmen and small manufacturers into bankruptcy, they came in time to exert an undue influence on the federal government. In the closing decade of the nineteenth century, the Senate was spoken of as "America's most exclusive millionaires' club." Many of its members represented, not the people who had elected them, but the giant corporations who had helped finance their campaigns.

In 1890, in response to popular discontent with this situation, Congress passed the Sherman Anti-trust Act. This law empowered the federal government to regulate the trusts and to ask the courts to break up those found guilty of restraint of trade. At first the leaders of American industry were untroubled. One of them expressed the confidence of his class by asserting: "Surely no President will ever stoop so low as to try to enforce the Sherman Anti-trust Act."

Theodore Roosevelt stooped. He had been in office only a few months when in February of 1902 he ordered his Attorney General to bring suit against the Northern Securities Company, a trust created by a group of industrialists and bankers to manage some Western railroads. Two years later the Supreme Court ruled in favor of the government, and Northern Securities became the first monopoly to be dissolved under the provisions of the Sherman Anti-trust Act. Thirty-nine other suits followed. The government won some, the trusts won the others.

The buoyant young man in the White House was not against Big Business in itself. At the turn of the century, the United States had 75 million people, more than double the number in Lincoln's day. Theodore Roosevelt realized that the goods needed by a constantly growing population could not be supplied by small economic entities alone. The larger economic entities—the corporations and trusts—had become a necessity.

His major accomplishment as President was not the dissolution of a few trusts—actually, more new ones were organized during his administration than during any other comparable period prior to the First World War. His major accomplishment was the firm establishment of the principle that the federal government had not only the right but the duty to examine the practices of large commercial units and to regulate them in the public interest.

With this goal in view, T.R. persuaded Congress to enact measures calling for federal meat inspection, a pure food and drug law, welfare laws for the residents of the District of Columbia, and a number of conservation laws. He also called for and got a new Cabinet-level federal department, that of Commerce and Labor. In June of 1902 he signed one of the most significant laws in recent American history, the Reclamation Act. Under its terms, citizens in the arid regions of the country could obtain federal aid in irrigating their lands. This development was to do as much for the

American West in Teddy's century as the California gold rush had done for it the century before.

Well before the completion of Roosevelt's first term, it was a common assumption that he was going to be the first President elevated from the Vice Presidency to be elected President on his own. Most Americans, to use his favorite expression, were "dee-lighted" with him. They liked his spunk, his wit, his daring, his unrelenting if not always successful effort to understand their problems and to do all he could about them. In the national election of 1904, both his popular majority (2½ million) and his electoral majority (336 to his Democratic opponent's 140) broke records; and his second induction into office was more joyfully anticipated by the people than any other presidential inauguration.

☆ ☆ ☆

With a population of 218,196, Teddy Roosevelt's Washington was more than twice the size of Lincoln's Washington. It was also far more pretentious. Well underway were the efforts to beautify the city in accordance with the plans drawn up a century before by George Washington's architect, Pierre L'Enfant.

Just east of the Capitol, on land once occupied by the hotel that had rocked to the rhythms of the first inaugural ball, the first of what are now the two huge buildings of the Library of Congress presented its pleasantly garish Italian Renaissance façade. North and South of the Capitol, two marble palaces were rising: an office building for the Senators, another for the Representatives. Heretofore the members of Congress had worked in their homes or rented commercial space downtown or, like Lincoln in his Congressional days, had carried their "offices" in their hats.

At the foot of Capitol Hill, business was still being conducted in the Pennsylvania Railroad's stone depot, whose heavy towers looked down on a raddle of train sheds and tracks. But these unsightly features of the Mall were soon to go. A few blocks to the northeast, the present elaborately fronted Union Station was halfway up.

The southern side of Pennsylvania Avenue, once a forlorn vista of warehouses, open markets, and frame shops, was beginning to take on its present neo-classic look with the near completion of the District Building at Fourteenth Street. The horse-drawn trolleys, first put into operation during Lincoln's time, still rattled down the center of the avenue. The horse-drawn carriage was still the staple of its traffic, although here and there one could spot a curiously constructed and noisy vehicle powered by a gasoline engine. Like most Americans, most Washingtonians regarded the horseless carriage as a passing fad. They would have been startled to learn that twenty-five years hence the horse would be as much a novelty on Pennsylvania Avenue as the automobile now was.

On the morning of Saturday, March 4, 1905, it looked for a while as though President Roosevelt's smile had taken over the skies. The sun was bright, the air balmy. Late in the morning there was a sudden reversal. Dark clouds gathered, hinting at rain or snow. A wild wind slapped in from the northwest. Before the swearing-in ceremonies could begin, the clouds vanished and the sun returned, but the wind remained. Cold, damp, and shrill, it tore at the banners fluttering from every lamppost and at the bunting draped from every building along the parade route.

At 10 a.m. the President made his way to the Capitol to do what every President does during the closing hours of a term—sign the last-minute bills passed by the retiring Congress. With him in his carriage were the members of his family: his second wife, the gracious Edith Carow Roosevelt; the charming and witty daughter of his first marriage, twenty-one-year-old Alice, whose wedding in the White House a year later would make her the socially prominent Mrs. Nicholas Longworth; the four young sons and one daughter of his present marriage. In the carriage behind rode the Vice President-elect, Charles Warren Fairbanks, a wealthy railroad lawyer from Indiana.

Progress was slow. The avenue was awash with tumultuously cheering people. The era of publicity, that vulgar assault on American privacy, was about to burst. As the presidential party moved toward Capitol Hill, newspaper photographers swarmed around. At one point the President instructed the Secret Service men who were guarding him to keep them at a distance so as to clear a path for his horsedrawn carriage.

Not since Andrew Jackson had a President ridden along Pennsylvania Avenue so certain of his place in the hearts of the voters. No doubt, much of Teddy Roosevelt's popularity was due to the degree to which his personality conformed to the spirit of his day. Not that his America was lacking in troubles. Only a decade before, a shy and unobtrusive Ohio sand-quarry operator named Jacob S. Coxey had led an "army" of four hundred men to Washington, demanding a public-works program of building to provide jobs for the unemployed. Everywhere there were individuals who were convinced that the only hope for the "have-nots" of the nation lay in the dubious financial reforms advocated by William Jennings Bryan, leader of the Democratic Party.

But these sounds of discontent were not the dominant note. Never before, and never since, have the American people, taken as a whole, been so bumptious, so optimistic, so sure of themselves. The fruits of the Industrial Revolution were just beginning to permeate the land. Building contractors were running advertisements in the press slyly pointing out the "social éclat"—not to mention the comfort—awaiting the homeowner who "*dared*" to put "a *second* bathroom in his house." It was the era of the bicycle built for two, of the mannish shirtwaist for women, of the Gibson girl and the Gibson man, of ragtime and the cakewalk.

The Americans of 1905 would have thought twice about putting into the White House a philosopher such as Jefferson or an introspective thinker such as Abraham Lincoln. But the husky and rather handsome man who stood doffing his hat to the shouting crowd as his carriage bore him up Pennsylvania Avenue on that gusty March morning was the apple of their eyes. In his bouncy and confident person they saw themselves writ large.

By the time he reached the Capitol, the plaza in front of the east portico was black with people, held well back from the building by a police rope barrier. As Teddy mounted the broad steps of the Senate wing, he stopped at frequent intervals to turn, flash his famous smile, and wave his top hat.

Of the inaugural ceremonies that began an hour later in

the Senate with the swearing-in of Fairbanks and then moved to the east portico for the presidential oath-taking and address, the Washington *Post* had this to say:

"It was Teddy's day! For him and him alone were the plaudits of a happy and enthusiastic people, the air echoing with the music of many bands, the wealth of decorations. . . . The curiosity regarding him was something phenomenal. His personality, forceful and original, dwarfed everything else. There was no interest in the proceedings in the Senate chamber until he appeared. The scene upon the inaugural stand lacked completeness until he came upon it. The procession commanded attention simply as the background against which his dominating individuality was outlined. The ball was attended by thousands whose presence was inspired by the fact that they would see him face to face."

☆ ☆ ☆

The inaugural address was brief and unconventional in form. It contained no concrete proposals for Congressional action. Like most Presidents succeeding themselves, Roosevelt preferred to withhold such suggestions until the time came to send his State of the Union message to Congress.

The first half of the address dealt in a general way with foreign affairs; the second dealt in the same manner with domestic ones. The gist of both was that the country had stepped not only into a new century but into a new era—the modern era.

The message had its prophetic passages. "We wish peace," said Roosevelt, "but we wish the peace of justice, the peace of righteousness. . . ."

Even as these words were spoken, the uneasy peace of Europe, broken since the Napoleonic Wars only by a few limited conflicts, was facing greater jeopardy than hardly anyone yet realized. As the result of a series of nineteenth-century border changes, millions of Europeans were living under governments for whom they felt neither loyalty nor affection. Abetting this dangerous situation was the growing ambitiousness of Germany, whose literature in the early twentieth century was rife with the theme that the people of the Fatherland were a superior race destined to dominate.

Well before the end of the decade following Teddy Roosevelt's second inauguration, the struggle for power among the major nations of Europe had divided the Old World into two armed camps. Bestride the heart of the continent was the Triple Alliance, later known as the Axis or the Central Powers, headed by Germany and what one worried observer called "the ramshackle empire" of Austria-Hungary. Dominating the outer edges of Europe was the Triple Entente, later known as the Allies or the Allied Powers, headed by Britain, France, and Russia.

To the seething mass of antagonisms that had created this division, the assassination on June 28, 1914, of the heir to the Austrian throne while on a state visit to Serbia was a match to a powder keg. Supported by Germany, Austria-Hungary declared war on little Serbia. Serbia's friends, Russia, France, and England, came to her aid in that order.

World War I was underway.

7

"We are provincials no longer"

☆ ☆ ☆

WOODROW WILSON

When all Europe burst into flame, Theodore Roosevelt was at his Long Island home, writing magazine articles, providing national leadership for the recently formed liberal branch of the Republican Party known as the Progressive Bull Moose wing, and recovering from a nearly fatal fever suffered during his recent exploration of a river that now bears his name in the jungles of Brazil. The man who had succeeded him in the Presidency, William Howard Taft, was teaching law at Yale; and the man who had succeeded Taft, Woodrow Wilson of New Jersey, was in the White House.

Tall, homely, long-jawed, Virginia-born Wilson had come into politics at the relatively late age of fifty-three after a distinguished career as historian, political scientist, and educator. Named to the presidency of Princeton University in 1902, he had startled the academic world by his efforts to make sweeping changes in the scholastic and social practices of the 156-year-old New Jersey school. Not all of his innovations were successful. Those that were, his efforts to elevate the university's teaching standards, were not universally appreciated. Accustomed to thinking of Princeton as little more than a finishing school for young gentlemen, one unhappy student remarked that "this place is getting to be nothing but a damned educational institution."

Eight years later, Wilson again demonstrated his capacity to startle and annoy. In 1910 the Democratic bosses of New Jersey prevailed on him to resign from Princeton and run for governor on a platform calling for badly needed reforms in the political and economic policies of the state. The bosses were not really interested in the reforms. Their only real interest was in seizing control of the New Jersey state House for their party. Their choice of Wilson was dictated by his reputation for honesty and high ideals. They assumed that he would give eloquent lip service to the reform movement during the campaign and then forget all about it when he was elected.

They were justified in this hope by Wilson's past pronouncements. His political views, as expressed in his many books, were on the conservative side. What the Democratic bosses failed to grasp was that Wilson was experiencing a change of heart, as indicated by his effort to infuse more democracy into the social life of Princeton.

Stepping from the quiet of the academic cloisters into the tumult of the political world, he soon sensed that the theories in his books were no answer to the problems of the common people of New Jersey. Great was the chagrin of the party bosses when on becoming governor he shook off their hold on him by making good on his campaign promises. Great was their astonishment when only two years later he became the first Democrat in twenty years to be elected President of the United States.

In the Presidency, as in the governorship, the schoolmaster-turned-statesman vigorously championed the cause of those millions of Americans who were not yet enjoying their share of the benefits of the Industrial Revolution—the working men and their unions, the small businessmen and their trade associations, the farmers of the North and West, the planters of the South. Under Wilson's New Freedom program, the country took greater strides in the direction of economic democracy than it had ever taken before or would take again until the days of Franklin Roosevelt and his New Deal. Out of the hopper of Congress came a host of progressive measures: a federal child-labor law, an act providing an eight-hour day for railroad workers, an act making credit more readily available to financially hard-pressed farmers.

Smoothing the path for the New Freedom were two amendments to the Constitution proposed by Congress under President Taft and ratified in 1913.

The sixteenth amendment permitted the federal government to collect taxes on the incomes of American citizens. By supplying the general government with a vast new source of revenue, the income-tax amendment made it easier for Wilson to obtain the first substantial reduction in the tariff since the Civil War. Every political change pleases one group and irks another. Chief beneficiaries of the Underwood-Simmons Tariff of 1914 were the consuming public, the small businessman, and the farmer. Its chief victims were the larger commercial interests, which were supported by Old Guard Republicanism.

The seventeenth amendment, providing for the direct popular election of United States Senators, had the effect of lessening the influence of Big Business on the upper house of Congress.

To translate his domestic program into law, Wilson took full advantage of these changes in the Constitution. His methods were adept and unique. He launched the New Freedom by reading his first State of the Union Message to a joint session of the Houses of Congress, thus becoming the first President since John Adams to communicate his recommendations to the legislature in person. He also took advantage of the increasing efficiency of America's newspapers and other communications media. To a degree never attempted by any previous President he developed the art of overcoming Congressional resistance to his proposals by making direct appeals for their support to the American people.

"It would be the irony of fate," he had remarked on the eve of his first inauguration, "if my administration had to deal chiefly with foreign affairs." With his mind concentrated on internal reforms, he was not well prepared to cope with the nagging foreign problems that arose almost at the start of his administration. Revolution and civil war in Mexico, friction with Colombia over the way the United States had acquired the Panama Canal Zone, friction with Japan over the treatment of Japanese in California—his handling of these and other foreign complications were not as satisfactory to the public or, generally speaking, as beneficial to the nation as his domestic strategy.

Difficult as these international problems were, they were trifling compared with what was to come. After 1914, they —and ultimately Wilson's domestic program as well—were cast into the shade by the overwhelming impact on American life and feeling of the conflict sparked across the Atlantic by the assassination of the heir to the throne of the rotting empire of Austria-Hungary.

Recent American history offers few events more charged with anxiety and confusion than those which little by little pushed the United States into World War I. On August 19, 1914, Wilson issued a proclamation of neutrality. This was acceptable to the American people. What was not acceptable was the President's plea that they remain neutral in their hearts. This was humanly impossible in a nation of immigrants, millions of whom had close personal ties with the countries on both sides of the conflict in the Old World.

For a while American sympathies were fairly evenly divided between Germany and the other Central Powers and England and her Allies. Then the troops of the German Emperor, Kaiser William II, goose-stepped into Belgium. Exaggerated stories of German cruelty filled the American press, and a surge of pro-Ally sympathy swept the country.

As of 1914, the United States had become the world's greatest producers of most of the products required by the warring forces—foodstuffs, raw textiles, iron, steel, and petroleum. In peacetime this country had carried on a profitable trade in these goods with all the nations of Europe. As the Great War got underway, efforts to continue this trade were hampered by the refusal of both England and Germany to respect America's right as a neutral to send her ships wherever she wished.

England blockaded the ports through which goods could be delivered to Germany. Germany retaliated by sending submarines into the Atlantic with the announcement that all ships traveling within a specified zone would be torpedoed without warning.

England's blockade excited groans, but it killed no Americans. Germany's submarines did. On May 7, 1915, the *Lusitania,* a British transatlantic liner, was sent to the bottom by a German torpedo. Of the 1,198 persons who lost their lives, 128 were Americans. In the United States, increasingly larger numbers of citizens began saying the government should declare war on Germany. This sentiment soon died down, only to revive for short intervals when more Americans perished in submarine attacks and several acts of espionage and sabotage by Germans in the United States came to light.

Official protests went from Washington to Berlin. They were not without effect. The autumn of 1915 brought a German promise to abandon unrestricted submarine warfare.

Even during the relative calm that followed, the question of whether the United States should enter the war on the side of England continued to agitate the American people. Only two sections of the population knew precisely where they stood—the extreme pacifists headed by William Jennings Bryan and a small but violently pro-war party, whose most articulate spokesman was Theodore Roosevelt. Outside of these two groups, one clamoring for peace at any price and the other for war without delay, opinion fluctuated with the daily newspaper headlines.

It was still fluctuating when the presidential election of 1916 got underway. Wilson's Republican opponent was the distinguished associate justice of the Supreme Court, Charles Evans Hughes of New York. The war permeated campaign oratory. The real issue, however—whether we should enter it—was never clearly presented to the electorate because the views of the major candidates were so close that Teddy Roosevelt scornfully described handsomely bearded Hughes as "a bewhiskered Wilson." Both candidates endorsed neutrality. Both expressed approval of a recent act of Congress under which the armed forces of the country had been increased, just in case.

The results were close, too—so close that not until the last votes were counted in the Far West, four days after the election, was Wilson's victory confirmed.

Many historians believe that what tipped the scale for the Democrats was a little phrase in their political platform. The plank in which this phrase was embedded extolled Wilson for the foreign policies he had pursued during his first term. It concluded with the statement, "He kept us out of war!"

That phrase was his party's rallying cry throughout the campaign. Apparently it was especially appealing to the women, for the election was decided in the West, where several states had recently granted the vote to their women citizens. The President himself did not like it. "They talk of me as though I were a god," he complained to his friend the Secretary of the Navy, Josephus Daniels. "Any little German lieutenant can put us into the war at any time by some calculated outrage."

His words were a forecast of coming events. During the four months between election day and the opening of Wilson's second term, Germany resumed unrestricted submarine warfare. As the quadrennial swearing-in ceremonies drew near, the crowds converging on Washington braced themselves for the grimmest inauguration since the days of Abraham Lincoln.

☆ ☆ ☆

Inauguration day, March 4, 1917, fell on a Sunday, with the public festivities scheduled for the following day. The President was sworn in twice. The first ceremony was held Sunday noon in the President's room at the National Capitol, whence Wilson had come from the White House with his family and members of his Cabinet. His reasoning was that, with the international situation becoming more tense by the moment, it would be unwise to leave the country without a Chief Executive for the next twenty-four hours.

Although the eyes of the country were fixed on strife-torn Europe, the United States was not without its domestic issues. The struggle of the women of America for the vote, begun back in 1848, was in its closing phase. In twelve states, most of them in the progressive West, women had won the vote. Now, under the banners of the National Woman's Party and other organizations, they were pounding on the doors of Congress. They wanted an amendment to the Federal Constitution that would do for them what the fifteenth amendment had done for Negro men.

Although aware that the women voters of the West had helped re-elect him, Wilson had not yet brought himself to endorse their movement. Intellectually a progressive, emotionally he was still a conservative. Brought up in a Presbyterian manse, under the eye of a brilliant but morally demanding minister-father, he looked on the members of the other sex as at least semi-divine. The thought of those "lovely creatures," as he called them, "soiling themselves in the mires of politics" was more than he could bear.

The day was close when he would change his mind and become a champion of the drive that in 1920 brought the nineteenth amendment, the woman's suffrage amendment, into the Constitution. But in 1917 he was still taking refuge in a legal technicality. Under the Constitution, the decision as to who could vote was left to the states. If the states wished their women citizens to have the ballot, well and good; but the question was not one with which the federal government should concern itself.

Four years earlier, on the day before his first inauguration, in 1913, the suffragettes had demonstrated in Washington. Five thousand of them had marched down Pennsylvania Avenue in a dawn-to-dusk parade, stepping to the cheers—and jeers—of forty thousand onlookers.

In the late afternoon a gang of disgruntled and drunken men had broken through the police line and disrupted the procession. Women were thrown to the pavement. Some were parted from their garments. At the recently built Daughters of the American Revolution Memorial Constitution Hall that evening, what had been planned as a victory rally became a protest meeting. In the House of Representatives, an elderly member reflected the sentiments of many of his colleagues by asserting that "the old hens should have stayed at home." Later, popular pressure forced a Congressional investigation, during which the details of the shameful incident were pictured to the world by angry women on the witness stand.

In 1917 the suffragettes were back in Washington, this time for a three-day convention during which two of their largest organizations, the Congressional Union for Woman's Suffrage and the National Woman's Party, were merged. For six weeks prior to the convention, women pickets could be seen strolling back and forth on Pennsylvania Avenue in front of the wrought-iron fence guarding the presidential lawns. Coming and going from his home, the President unfailingly favored them with a broad smile and a polite lift of his hat as his carriage bore him through the White House gates.

Plans called for the convention to conclude its business on Sunday, March 4 with a giant demonstration. As originally conceived, this demonstration was to be carried out in imitation of the march of the ancient Israelites around the walls of the city of Jericho in the Palestinian valley of the Jordan River. According to the Old Testament, the Israelites captured Jericho from its Canaanite rulers by a combination of movement and sound. Carrying the Ark of God and having marched around Jericho seven times, the Israelites blew on their rams' horns, whereupon the walls of the city fell.

Like the Israelites, the suffragettes, a thousand of them

in all, were to encircle the White House seven times, carrying with them what they called the "suffrage ark" and "accompanied by the long blast of the ram's horn." At the last minute these dramatic plans were modified in the face of widely voiced objections. One was that, because of the war scare, such militant behavior might be unseemly. It was thought, too, that some people might consider the affair a little sacrilegious. In the end the ladies, assembling at three in the afternoon, contented themselves with moving around the White House a couple of times, so dressed and arranged as to create a moving chain of purple, white, and gold.

A great crowd was on hand to watch them, for by March 4 the city was swarming with out-of-towners come to take part in the festivities of the following day. The Sunday issue of the Washington *Post* mirrored their concerns. Huge scareheads covered a lead story dealing with the recent exposure of a secret German offer, in the event of United States participation in the war, to form an alliance with Mexico for the purpose of seizing the American Southwest.

Every inch of the front page was devoted to the war, except for one large and two small stories. The large story offered a preview of tomorrow's inauguration ceremonies. One of the small stories pictured the traffic snarl in the city during the rain of the night before when, just as the after-theater crowds were struggling to get home, two streetcars had collided on New York Avenue. The third story recorded the efforts of the Texas House of Representatives to impeach Governor James E. ("Pa") Ferguson for misappropriation of state funds.

On page seven was a headline that for today's reader is

full of nostalgia: "Anti-Suffragists Open Tea Rooms." Some of the local ladies, members of the Association Opposed to Woman Suffrage, shared the President's distaste at the thought of women in politics. Those who wished to hear their side of the argument could do so at 1215 Pennsylvania Avenue in an "arbor-like" lounge "tastefully decorated with American flags, foliage and pink roses." Open to the public throughout inauguration week, the combination restaurant and tea room featured luncheons "at a modest charge" and free coffee.

☆ ☆ ☆

At dawn on Monday the weather was clear but far from comfortable. During the early morning hours, low rain clouds swept the sky. These disappeared shortly before noon, but the sun which prevailed for the remainder of the day was marred by a 36-mile-an-hour gale that rapidly lowered temperatures to a point below freezing.

Thick crowds had been standing along the parade route for hours when at eleven in the morning Wilson left the White House to ride to the Capitol with his second wife, the last President to make this historic journey in a horse-drawn vehicle.

En route to the Capitol and later on the return trip to the White House, the presidential carriage was accompanied by closely formed lines of soldiers armed with loaded guns. Not since March 4, 1861, had such extensive precautions been taken to protect a President-elect. From the roofs of the buildings along the avenue, more than a hundred special detectives kept close scrutiny on the throngs below. Near both the inaugural stand at the Capitol and the reviewing stand in the Court of Honor in front of the White House, machine guns capable of discharging eight hundred shots a minute were in position.

In accordance with a custom that was to prevail until the second inauguration of Franklin Roosevelt, Vice President Thomas R. Marshall of Indiana, re-elected with Wilson, took his oath in the Senate chamber. At the end of this ceremony, the presidential party moved to the pillared wooden platform above the recently rebuilt granite steps of the east front of the Capitol, where Wilson was sworn in and delivered his address.

Only briefly did the President touch on the domestic accomplishments of his first term. "Perhaps no equal period in our history," he said, fairly enough, "has been so fruitful of important reforms. . . . We have sought very thoughtfully to set our house in order, correct the grosser errors and abuses of our industrial life, liberate and quicken the processes of our national genius and energy, and lift our politics to a broader view of the people's essential interests."

Practically all the rest of the speech dealt with the crisis abroad. Through every passage ran the clear implication that what was now Europe's war would soon be America's war too.

"We are provincials no longer," Wilson told his forty thousand listeners, some of whom, unable to get a good view of him from the plaza or on the grounds in front of the Capitol, had taken up positions on the lawns of the Library of Congress across the street. "The tragic events of the thirty months of vital turmoil through which we have just passed have made us citizens of the world. There can be no turning back. Our own fortunes as a nation are involved whether we would have it so or not."

Starting at 1:30, the parade lasted for two and a half hours. At the beginning, the wooden bleachers lining the avenue were crowded, but the winds were biting, and by the time the parade ended, the bleachers were half empty. A sheet of plate glass protected the President and his party on the reviewing stand.

Wilson stood throughout most of the ceremony. He smiled, removed his hat, and bowed deeply as the thousand suffragettes who had encircled the White House the day before marched by, the first women to take part in an inaugural parade. In recent months military preparedness—"armed neutrality," it was called—had become one of the keynotes of American life. With it had arisen a fervent patriotism. Of this there were many evidences in the passing pageant. In the "Americanization section" marched thousands of "new citizens," representing every one of the many nationalities that then, as now, made up the population of the United States. Their waving banners carried the slogan "America First," and identified their bearers as Roumanians, Italians, Serbs, Poles, and so forth. Wilson's eyes misted when past the reviewing stand went several hundred aging veterans of the Civil War, carrying a streamer inscribed: "G.A.R. (Grand Army of the Republic). Ready for Duty."

In the evening, notwithstanding the bitter cold, a huge crowd gathered at the Washington Monument to witness what the *Post* described as a "brilliant pyrotechnical display." Thousands strolled through the Court of Honor, lighted for the benefit of visitors.

Next morning's *Post* carried a little item prophetic of what was to be one of the uglier aspects of World War I—the tendency of Americans to distrust fellow Americans of German descent. The newspaper reported that in Boston one August von Hagen was being held in $5,000 bail. An American-born mechanic, von Hagen was charged with having used a small American flag to wipe the grease spots from his workbench.

☆ ☆ ☆

A month later the United States took her place in the war, not as an "ally" but as an "associated power," alongside England, France, and Italy, and their friends. On April 6, 1917, the date of this country's official declaration of war, the armed forces of America numbered only 200,000. Within the next twenty months, more than four million young men, most of them drafted, were put into uniform and trained. More than two million were sent overseas, and 1,390,000 saw active combat in Europe.

In the opening month of the following year, Wilson issued his famous Fourteen Points, a list of the conditions under which he hoped peace could eventually be negotiated with Germany and the other Axis Powers. In essence, the Fourteen Points embodied President Wilson's vision of the kind of world he wanted to see arise from the ashes of war.

Among other things, he called for the use of the principle of self-determination in settling the complaints of colonial peoples and others living under governments they did not like. His fourteenth and most celebrated point envisaged the establishment after the war of an international peace-keeping organization, later referred to as the League of Nations.

The war ended with the signing of the Armistice on November 11, 1918, and in December Wilson sailed to Europe to participate personally in drafting the terms of peace. The Treaty of Versailles, as the terms of peace were named, was framed by the "Big Four": Wilson for the United States, Georges Clemenceau for France, David Lloyd George for Great Britain, and Vittorio Orlando for Italy. In two series of negotiations in Paris, Wilson struggled to persuade his fellow peacemakers to base the treaty on his Fourteen Points. His major determination was to have the Covenant of the proposed League of Nations included as an integral part of the treaty, with the understanding that those victor nations whose governments accepted the treaty would automatically become members of the League.

In this effort he succeeded, but to gain his point he was forced to make many concessions with regard to the remaining peace terms. Consequently, the Treaty of Versailles placed far harsher demands on Germany and the other defeated nations than would have been so had it been based entirely on the Fourteen Points. The necessary signatures were placed on the treaty in the summer of 1919, and Wilson returned to the United States, where disappointment and tragedy awaited him.

☆ ☆ ☆

Under the Constitution no treaty can take effect without the approval of the Senate, and since the elections of the year before, the Senate had been in Republican hands. This situation alone, however, was not responsible for the failure of the United States to sign the Treaty of Versailles and become a member of the League of Nations.

Where the treaty, or more precisely, our entry into the League was concerned, the Senate Republican majority was split into two camps—the Moderates headed by Henry Cabot Lodge of Massachusetts, and the Irreconcilables headed by Hiram W. Johnson of California, William E. Borah of Idaho, and Robert LaFollette of Wisconsin. The Moderates favored American participation in the League, provided some reservations were incorporated in the League Covenant to protect traditional American interests. The Irreconcilables opposed participation under any conditions.

As what promised to be a long hard fight broke out in the Senate, the President embarked on a speaking tour to enlist popular support for his position. Response to his appearances was good. His strategy might have succeeded had he been able to complete his tour. But this was not to be.

The strain of the negotiations in Paris had undermined his health. Sixty-two-year-old Wilson was not a well man when he left Washington in September of 1919. In the course of traveling 9,500 miles in twenty-one days, and of delivering thirty-seven speeches in twenty-nine cities, he suffered frequently from migraine and other ills. On September 25, at Pueblo, Colorado, he collapsed and was rushed back to Washington. There, on October 2, he suffered a stroke that incapacitated him during the crucial period that followed.

Meanwhile the debate in the Senate droned on. Little by little, the Democrats and the Republican Moderates joined hands to hammer out a compromise that reduced what were originally forty-three reservations to the League Covenant to fourteen. By November 6, Senator Lodge, as chairman of the Foreign Relations Committee, was able to inform the President that the Senate stood ready to ratify the Treaty of Versailles and the League Covenant with the fourteen reservations. Although the reservations would not have seriously weakened American participation in the League, they were not acceptable to the sick man in the White House. His instructions to his Democratic followers in the Senate, delivered by letter on November 18, were to vote for the Treaty and the League Covenant exactly as they were when he had brought them home from Paris, or for nothing at all.

The result—nothing at all. The United States concluded separate treaties with its erstwhile World War I enemies, and the American people put the lofty aims of the Wilson Era behind them to revel in the fleshpots of the Roaring Twenties, a hectic interlude that began with the accession of Harding to the Presidency in 1921 and ended less than a decade later with the onset of the Great Depression and the emergence of Franklin Delano Roosevelt.

8

"I want to talk with the people"

☆ ☆ ☆

FRANKLIN D. ROOSEVELT

According to the Superintendent of Police of the District of Columbia, the inauguration crowds in 1933 were the largest to date. According to reporters come from all over the world to cover the festivities in Washington, they were the quietest.

Cheering there was, as always, but it was muted. Movement there was, but the Washington *Herald* found it "frighteningly mechanical in contrast to the joyous abandon usually associated with inauguration-day assemblages."

Responsible for this subdued atmosphere were events of the preceding decade. Familiar though these events are, some of them must be reviewed to give a clear appreciation of the problems confronting Franklin Delano Roosevelt, the man with the powerful shoulders, the clear blue-gray eyes, the electrifying smile, and the habit of throwing up his strong chin, whom the people had summoned to the Presidency by a landslide vote in the election of the previous November.

☆ ☆ ☆

At the end of World War I, the refusal of the United States to finish its job in Europe by joining the League of Nations had a profound effect on the American people. Throughout the country there rose a cry for a return to "normalcy," meaning, as it turned out, to a form of isolationism that was a caricature of the judicious neutrality urged upon his countrymen by George Washington over a century before. A people who in 1917 had thrilled to Woodrow Wilson's call "to make the world safe for democracy" now decided that their salvation lay in letting the rest of the world go hang.

Into the vacuum created by the failure of Wilsonian idealism rolled a rabid materialism. At its frenetic height, the Jazz Age of the 1920's found the American people more preoccupied with moneymaking and pleasure than at any time before. It was the age of the flapper and the Charleston, of a swiftly rising stock market shedding what the historians Charles and Mary Beard called "a golden glow" over what to the generality of Americans appeared to be an economic paradise without end or limits.

Contributing to this mindless merry-go-round was the eighteenth amendment, the prohibition amendment, added to the Constitution in 1918. The intent of the amendment was to do away with "the evils of the saloon" and to shower the country with the blessings of alcoholic abstinence. Unfortunately, law has inherent limitations. A law is not what we want it to do, but what it can do. The eighteenth amendment, repealed in 1933, now stands as a monument to the impossibility of regulating the drinking habits of a nation by governmental edict.

America had always been a hard-drinking country, but prior to prohibition heavy consumption of spirits had been confined largely to the male population. With the coming of prohibition, women as well as men bragged about their personal bootleggers and frequented the speak-easy, showplace of the great new American industry, organized crime. American storytellers have romanticized the Jazz Age. American movies have glamorized its lighter side, but we know now that all through the twenties the country was laughing and drinking its way into catastrophe.

Immediately after World War I, the country suffered an economic recession as the American industrial machine, geared to meet the huge demands of war, reorganized to meet the lesser ones of peace. For the farmers and a few other elements of the population the recession went on and on, but for those dependent on the associated worlds of commerce and manufacturing and finance, recovery was swift and thorough.

Soon, all over the country, people were clamoring for the privilege of buying shares in the industries of a free-enterprise system that appeared to be prospering as never before. Previously speculation on the stock market had been carried on almost exclusively by professionals who understood the risks involved. Now all sorts of people were buying stocks. Since most of them had only modest resources, they had to buy on credit—which meant that the difference between what they had paid for their stocks and what they still owed on them was so great that unless the stock market continued to go up and up, they could be wiped out in a minute.

Signs of impending disaster were plentiful, but most people were too blinded by the golden glow to notice them. Those who pointed them out were ignored. The first unmistakable indication that the "boom" was over came in October of 1929, when the stock market crashed, putting literally millions of Americans on the road to financial ruin.

The ensuing economic depression seemed for a while to be practically without bottom. Its physical deprivations were hard enough. Its psychological impact was even worse. All through the boom, the American people had listened reverently to the gospel of the twenties as summed up in the laconic words of President Coolidge: "The business of America is business." In the grueling depths of the depression they awakened to the realization that their idol, business, had somehow failed them.

A physical silence settled over the land as the factories closed and their wheels stopped turning. A spiritual silence succeeded it as the people struggled in vain to give a name to the evil they felt was stalking among them, painfully aware that an enemy that cannot be seen cannot be fought.

Had Herbert Hoover, the occupant of the White House in the early 1930's, had the ability gently to tell the people that the evil was in them and that they themselves could eradicate it, his efforts to grapple with the depression might have worked. But although Hoover was a man of superior abilities and fine moral character, he was not adept at communicating with those who had elected him to office in the Republican triumph of 1928.

Long exploded is the once widely circulated legend of Hoover cowering in the White House and doing nothing while the depression raged. He did many things. He was hampered, however, by his conviction that direct governmental assistance to individuals would destroy the free-enterprise system and freedom itself. Such actions as he took were designed to help the people indirectly. By setting up the Reconstruction Finance Corporation and similar devices, he made financial aid available to the higher echelons of the free-enterprise system—principally to the larger corporations, which employ so many of the country's men and women. His theory, as explained by the press, was that the benefits bestowed on the higher units of the economy would eventually "dribble down" to the people.

In the long pull they might have done just that. But as one of Hoover's critics would later point out, "People do not eat in the long pull. They eat every day."

Unable to find in the White House the caliber of leadership the crisis demanded, the people looked for it elsewhere. As the presidential election of 1932 drew close, the eyes of millions of Americans were on fifty-year-old Franklin D. Roosevelt, who as Governor of New York since 1928 had cushioned the effects of the depression in that state by the establishment of an old-age pension and other measures designed to help individuals in need.

Named as the standard bearer of his party in July, Governor Roosevelt ignored the tradition that the nominee should await official notification of his selection. Instead, he flew from Albany to Chicago and thanked the Democratic convention in person.

"I pledge you, I pledge myself," he told the cheering delegates, "to a *new deal* for the American people."

Four months later, at the polls, the voters endorsed Roosevelt and his promised New Deal in such overwhelming numbers that in the electoral college he carried forty-two states as against Hoover's six.

During the closing months of Hoover's administration the situation worsened. By the first of the new year, twelve million Americans were unemployed. Bread lines were visible in cities, towns, and even villages across the land.

On March 1, 1933, as the President-elect journeyed from his home in Hyde Park to New York City, en route to Washington, black newspaper headlines revealed that the banks were closed in twelve states. Closures or restrictions on banking operations were expected momentarily throughout the nation.

Arriving in the capital on the somber rainy afternoon of Thursday, March 2, Roosevelt took quarters on the seventh floor of the Mayflower Hotel on Connecticut Avenue. He spent the evening working on his inaugural address. At his elbow lay a copy of the works of the nineteenth-century American essayist, Henry David Thoreau, who years before had written: "Nothing is so much to be feared as fear."

Although the President-elect appreciated the pertinence of Thoreau's thought to the current situation, he expressed surprise later at the favorable public reaction to the most quoted line of his address, his assertion that "the only thing we have to fear is fear itself—nameless, unreasoning, unjustified terror which paralyzes needed efforts to convert retreat into advance."

On the following day, Friday, he made his formal call on President Hoover at the White House. Several times, since the November election, Hoover had invited the President-elect to join him in measures that he believed would be helpful in retarding the depression. To these overtures Roosevelt had responded politely but guardedly, taking care to avoid any show of cooperation with the retiring President. Like Lincoln, he preferred to keep his plans for coping with the crisis to himself until such time as he had the power to act on them.

The Friday-afternoon meeting between the two men was brief and stiff. When it was over, Roosevelt hastened with relief to the Mayflower to spend his last night as President-elect with the members of his family who had accompanied him to Washington: his mother, Mrs. James Roosevelt of Hyde Park; his wife, the remarkable Eleanor Roosevelt; his daughter, Mrs. Anna Dall; and two of his four sons, married James and Harvard-bound John.

On Saturday the half a million people who had come to Washington to participate in the induction of the new President found their preoccupations lavishly reflected in the pages of the local newspapers.

The sports section of the *Herald* featured a cartoon illustrating the "amazing parallel" between the two presidential Roosevelts, Theodore and Franklin. Distantly related—fifth cousins, to be exact—both were seventh in descent from the first American member of the family, Klas Martensen van Roosevelt. Both were graduates of Harvard and Columbia University Law School. Both had been members of the New York legislature and both had been governors of that state. Both had been candidates for the Vice Presidency—Franklin unsuccessfully in 1920. Each had been shot at by a maniac—Theodore while campaigning unsuccessfully for the Presidency on the Bull Moose ticket in 1912, Franklin in Florida three months after his recent election.

A page-four headline underscored the continuing hold of prohibition: "Analysis of Inaugural Liquor Shows It Is Safe to Consume—Eight Samples Bought from Washington Bootleggers Proves [sic] Ample in Alcoholic Content But Mostly Synthetic."

A business-section headline pointed to a silver lining in the local economic cloud: "3 to 4 Million New Cash Here for Inaugural—Influx of Visitors with Money Expected to Boost Capital Trade above Recent Marks."

And a long and jingly editorial-page poem bemoaned the continuance of hard times.

The poem opened with a dirge:

The Capitol is draped in flags,
While those not present dress in rags.

It closed with a prayer:

Behold the Ides of March is here!
So let us shed a modest tear,
And give a cheer for Roosevelt's luck—
And, while the tourists crash the gates,
God save these same United States!

For Eleanor Roosevelt the morning began like any other. Shortly after seven she could be seen striding briskly down Connecticut Avenue, walking her small dog Maggie. A faint flush of sun in the gray sky when she left the hotel had disappeared by the time she returned. The temperature had started its slow climb to a mild forty-seven degrees. People curious to see her husband were already drifting into the hotel lobby, but it was another two hours before the President-elect put in an appearance there, his family with him. To the even larger crowds assembled beyond the entranceway, he waved cheerily from the wheel chair that bore him across the pavement to one of the two open touring cars waiting to take the Roosevelts to a ten-o'clock prayer service at St. John's Episcopal Church, the "Church of the Presidents," on the northern side of Lafayette Square.

A victim of poliomyelitis in his thirty-ninth year, Franklin Roosevelt had at first been paralyzed from the waist down but had regained the partial use of his legs by long and unremitting personal exertions. Even so, he could stand only by locking the heavy braces on his legs. He could walk only by leaning on a companion.

From St. John's the cars carried the Roosevelts around the square to the White House, and from there, shortly after eleven, the presidential party began its traditional progress to the Capitol. The outgoing and incoming Chief Executives rode together in an open car, escorted by a cavalry unit from Fort Meyer, Virginia. Their wives followed in another open car.

John Nance Garner of Texas had already gone to the Capitol, the last Vice President to take his oath in the Senate chamber. Since Roosevelt's second inauguration, four years later, the practice has been for the Vice President to be sworn in immediately in advance of the President on the platform above the steps of the east portico.

Beginning with Harding's inauguration in 1920, a public-address system had been used for the inaugural ceremonies at the Capitol, making it easier for the crowds to hear the President take his oath and deliver his address. On March 4, 1933, the 150,000 people waiting for Roosevelt in front of the east portico were entertained by a local radio announcer. He gave them a running commentary on the state —or rather the plight—of the Union. To this, when the time came, he added an account of the ceremonies taking place in the Senate chamber.

These ceremonies, beginning with the arrival of Roosevelt at one minute after noon, followed the usual order. First, Garner was sworn in, with retiring Vice President Charles Curtis administering the oath. Then Garner gave a brief talk without notes or manuscript. Curtis then delivered a short farewell address and at 12:08 declared the seventy-second Congress adjourned *sine die*. Then, pursuant to a proclamation recently issued by President Hoover, Garner immediately convened the new Senate and swore in its newly elected members.

The procession from Senate chamber to platform occupied more than half an hour, for Roosevelt insisted on walking through the crowded corridors, his arm linked through that of his son James. The first hint received by the crowds outside that the great event was about to begin came at 12:30 when a squad of soldiers and marines marched out of the building, carrying an American flag and the presidential flag, a blue banner with a white silken fringe. The servicemen took up positions at the base of the ivy-draped wooden platform. The flag, flying from the dome of the Capitol behind them, was at full height, but those on all the other public buildings in the city were at half mast for Senator Thomas J. Walsh of Montana, who had been scheduled to be Roosevelt's Attorney General but who had died on the previous Thursday.

Of the presidential party, Hoover was the first to appear on the platform. There were a few cheers. Gradually the platform filled up with top-hatted gentlemen and brilliantly gowned ladies. There was a moment of confusion as the new Secretary of Labor, Frances Perkins, first woman to be named to a presidential Cabinet, arrived late and encountered difficulties in reaching her appointed place. At the appearance of Roosevelt, the United States Marine Band executed four ruffles and then broke into the strains of "Hail to the Chief."

Roosevelt took his oath first and then delivered his address. His huge audience listened attentively but displayed few evidences of enthusiasm. Later that day the newspapers would make it clear that the thousands who heard him in person and the millions more who listened at their radio regarded his speech as to the point and effective. But the American people had lost their faith in words. For too many unhappy years they had been listening to Herbert Hoover telling them that prosperity was around a corner that no one had yet sighted. From the man they had elected to Hoover's place they expected more than words.

Only once was there a stir of consequence among those in front of the east portico. That was when the new President said: "Our greatest primary task is to put people to work. . . ." Otherwise, save for a little applause at the end, the inaugural crowd listened to the address in what several reporters described as a "deadly silence."

When Roosevelt had finished, Hoover shook hands with him and then departed with his wife to catch a train that would carry him to New York and a long rest. Mrs. Roosevelt sat beside her husband on the return trip to the White House. To reporters who sought her out after her arrival there, she gave her own graphic version of the swearing-in ceremony.

"It was very, very solemn," she said, "and a little terrifying. The crowds were so tremendous, and you felt that they would do anything—if only someone would tell them what to do."

At two o'clock the inaugural parade began to unfold in the vicinity of the Capitol. Headed by General Douglas MacArthur, Chief of Staff of the Army, and the Army band, it was no sooner underway than instructions arrived for it to hold up for twenty minutes. The President and his family needed the time to finish their lunch at the White House and repair to the reviewing stand in the Court of Honor, which had been designed to resemble the balcony of Federal Hall where George Washington had taken his oath as the first President a hundred and forty-four years before.

The parade lasted for almost three hours and was three miles long. It contained all of the usual elements—special military units, veterans of the American wars, groups of In-

dians, flower-bedecked floats, and fifty bands playing "The Franklin Delano Roosevelt March" composed by William H. Woodin, the newly designated Secretary of the Treasury.

The only really spontaneous ovations of the day were given to Al Smith, who marched at the head of the big New York contingent. Every appearance of the man Franklin Roosevelt had long ago labeled "The Happy Warrior of the Political Battlefield" excited the crowds lining the parade route and blocking the side streets leading into Pennsylvania Avenue. As the Democratic nominee four years before, Smith had opposed Hoover in a hard-fought election campaign sullied by a barrage of slander and innuendo directed at Smith by some of his opponents because of his adherence to the Roman Catholic faith. Although soundly defeated in 1928, the last year of the so-called "Republican boom," the bright and engaging New Yorker remained a popular figure.

The tragedy and the flimflam associated with all inaugurations were sufficiently in evidence to attract the attention of alert reporters. An aged woman died as she knelt in prayer for the new President. Sirens screamed all day long as ambulances rushed to the hospitals with persons suffering injuries ranging from fingers torn off by the propeller of an Army blimp used in the parade to heart attacks. An enterprising salesman relieved his own personal depression by hawking parade-bleacher tickets on which he had printed the words "Good for anywhere, signed by President Roosevelt." Another huckster shouted: "Here you are, folks, the greatest picture in American history, only twenty-five cents." Those who parted with their quarters got a snapshot of

Franklin Roosevelt. "Where's your overcoat?" one inauguration visitor asked another. "I just hocked it," was the reply, "so's I could celebrate the New Deal."

"This nation asks for action and action now . . . ," Roosevelt had said in his inaugural address. "We must act and act quickly."

Even before inauguration day was over, he was making good on this promise to take immediate steps to relieve the great depression. As people waltzed at the ball that evening or watched the traditional fireworks display, the new President and his aides were putting the New Deal underway.

On the following day, Sunday, Roosevelt ordered Congress into special session, issued a proclamation under his wartime powers closing the nation's banks for the next four days, and began work on an emergency bill designed to reopen them on a sound basis. When Congress convened as directed on Thursday, the lower House, where all financial measures must be initiated, organized quickly and began immediate consideration of a banking bill prepared by the President and his assistants during a literally sleepless seventy-two hours. Newly elected Congressmen were still wandering about the chamber looking for their seats when thirty-eight minutes later the House approved the bill by a unanimous vote. Three hours later the Senate had passed it. Roosevelt signed it into law that evening, and within the next fourteen days, fifty percent of the nation's banks, representing ninety percent of its banking deposits, had reopened.

On the following Sunday evening, the President went on the air to deliver the first of his "fireside chats." Franklin Roosevelt and radio were made for each other. His rich and carefully controlled voice, as it went out over the nation, exuded calm and optimism. His manner of delivery was dramatic without being pretentious, serious without being solemn.

In a physical sense, depression continued to plague the American economy until this country entered the Second World War eight years later. In a spiritual sense, the turning point for the better was reached that Sunday evening when the President seated himself in his White House office and said into the microphone on his desk: "I want to talk a few minutes with the people of the United States about banking."

Then, in simple language but without condescension, he explained the complicated steps taken during the previous week to meet the banking crisis. His closing words were an appeal for the confidence of the public.

He got it. To that the unprecedented avalanche of laudatory letters and telegrams into the White House during the next few days provided ample testimony.

From the banking crisis Congress turned to the other problems of the depression. By the time the special session was adjourned at the end of the famous "Hundred Days," on June 16, Congress had produced the largest single block of reform and relief legislation in American history.

Students of the Roosevelt Era tell us that there was not one New Deal, but three.

New Deal 1, begun during the Hundred Days and resumed in 1934, produced a body of emergency relief laws providing jobs for the unemployed and food for the hungry. It also produced the Agricultural Adjustment Act, designed to restore the purchasing power of American farmers. In addition it established the Federal Bank Deposit Insurance Corporation to prevent a repetition of the banking crisis of March 1933, and a regulatory body for the stock market to prevent a repetition of the crash of October 1929.

New Deal 2, launched shortly after the opening of Roosevelt's second term in 1937, brought forth among other things the giant job-giving organization known as the WPA (Work Projects Administration) and the Social Security Act, providing compensation for the unemployed and insurance for the aged.

New Deal 3, put underway late that same year, saw among other things the passage of a law designed to make it easier for low-income families to acquire adequate housing.

The passage of time has convinced many political observers that by no means all the New Deal legislation was justified or wise. Some aspects of it were ill-conceived. Some failed to achieve their stated ends. Some, declared unconstitutional by the Supreme Court, had to be revised to bring them into line with the basic law of the land. But whatever the shortcomings of the New Deal, nothing is ever likely to diminish the gratitude of the American people to the man who, taking over the Presidency at a moment of national peril, restored to them their faith in their economic system, in their political system, and in their ability to help themselves.

☆ ☆ ☆

Like Woodrow Wilson, Franklin D. Roosevelt began his administration with a concentration on domestic problems and ended it in the midst of an international disaster.

The most striking development in Europe between the

two world wars was the rise of the totalitarian dictatorships. The triumph of the Communists in Russia during the closing months of the First World War was followed in 1922 by the triumph of Benito Mussolini and the Fascists in Italy and the subsequent emergence of Adolf Hitler and the National Socialists in Germany.

Named Chancellor of the German Reich in 1933, the Nazi *Führer* dissolved the national legislature, arrogated all governmental powers to himself, and embarked on a devastating campaign of terror and expansion. In defiance of the Treaty of Versailles, under which the army of the Reich was limited to 100,000 men, he re-created the mammoth German war machine, occupied a section of his country legally under League of Nations supervision, and annexed Austria and Czechoslovakia.

Efforts by Prime Minister Neville Chamberlin of Britain to appease the German dictator only whetted his appetite for conquest and power. In the autumn of 1939 he sent his armies into Poland. Then it was—when England and France tried to come to Poland's aid—that the Second World War broke out.

For Nazi Germany the first eighteen months of the conflict were an unbroken series of victories. Denmark, Norway, the Netherlands, Belgium—one by one, these old nations of Western Europe fell under the German heel. In the early summer of 1940 a battered Anglo-French army of 300,000 men would have been annihilated had it not been for the action of the new Prime Minister of England, Winston Churchill, in effecting its evacuation from the French fishing port of Dunkirk.

France fell a few weeks later.

A turning point in the conflict was reached during the following fall, however, when England, in "her finest hour," repelled a massive German air offensive initiated in preparation for an invasion that never materialized. Unable to move west, *Der Führer* moved east. In June of 1941 he scrapped a two-year-old pact of alliance with the Soviet Union and sent his armies across the borders of Russia. Meanwhile Japan had joined the Axis, as the belligerents headed by Germany and Italy were known. On December 7, 1941, the Japanese air force attacked Pearl Harbor, the American naval base in Hawaii. On the following day the United States entered the war with England and the Soviet Union as her principal allies.

During World War II this country underwent a resurgence of Wilsonian idealism. In the summer of 1941 the allied war aims were presented to mankind in a document issued jointly by Roosevelt and Churchill and known as the Atlantic Charter. Like Wilson's Fourteen Points, the Atlantic Charter called for an end to military aggression and for the recognition of the principle of self-determination, under which every nation of the world would be forever free to choose its own rulers and its own form of government. To guarantee these high goals, the Charter also called for the creation after the war of a stronger version of the then practically defunct League of Nations.

Although this proposed peace-keeping body eventually took form as the United Nations, it had become clear well in advance of the capitulation of Germany that the Soviet Union was not in accord with the war aims of her English and American allies. On April 5, 1945, only slightly more than a month before the formal surrender of Germany,

Roosevelt dispatched a pathetic note to Joseph Vissariono-vich Stalin.

"It would be one of the great tragedies in history," he wrote the aging Russian leader, "if at the very moment of victory . . . distrust . . . and lack of faith should prejudice the entire undertaking after the colossal losses of life and material and treasure involved."

Seven days later Franklin Roosevelt was dead, and the problems connected with the ending of the war and the beginning of the peace were in the hands of his fourth-term Vice President, Harry S. Truman of Missouri.

☆ ☆ ☆

During the next few weeks Truman was called on to make one of the most fateful decisions in history. Secretly the United States had developed a weapon of terrifying power, the atomic bomb. Should it be used to bring Japan, still in the war, to her knees? The President's answer was made known to the world on August 6, 1945, when the bomb was dropped on the Japanese city of Hiroshima. Three days later a second atomic bomb devastated Nagasaki, and on August 14 Japan surrendered.

"Hot war" was followed by "cold war" when the Soviet Union, determined to prevent another invasion of her homeland by a European enemy, marched her armies into a half a dozen countries along her western borders. When the United States refused to recognize her right to seize and control these so-called satellites, the relationship between the one-time allies disintegrated. Millions of people who had hoped that the Second World War would produce one cooperating world found instead that it had produced two rival worlds—a Communist world and a free world, separated by what Churchill later described as "the iron curtain."

In February of 1947 the British ambassador in Washington called at the White House with unhappy news. Badly shaken economically by the war, Great Britain was no longer able to make good on her promises to provide economic and military assistance to Greece and Turkey. Unless these countries continued to receive help from the free world, they would have to seek it from the Soviet Union, and thus subject themselves to Communist control.

Again President Truman was required to take a fateful step. His decision to ask Congress to provide foreign aid to Greece and Turkey had the effect of shifting the burden of leadership in the free world from Great Britain to the United States.

Throughout the remainder of his administration, Truman endeavored to cope with the problems of a divided world by pursuing a policy of containment. Its objective was to confine Communist influence to those sections of the globe where it already existed, to keep it from spreading. In Europe, thanks to the Truman Doctrine and the giant foreign-aid program known as the Marshall Plan, the policy was an unqualified success. In Asia, this was not the case. There American efforts to keep China under the influence of the free world failed. In 1949 the Nationalist Chinese fled to the island of Formosa and the mainland of China fell under the control of Communist leaders.

During the administration of Harry Truman's successor in the White House, Dwight D. Eisenhower, American foreign policy was formulated for several years by his controversial Secretary of State, John Foster Dulles. Secretary Dulles took the position that the policy of containment was inadequate. The United States should make an actual effort to free the peoples of the satellite countries of Central Europe from their Communist overlords.

In 1956 Dulles's "policy of liberation" was challenged by uprisings in the satellite countries of Poland and Hungary. When the United States failed to intervene on the side of the Polish and Hungarian "freedom fighters," the policy of liberation had to be put aside as so much empty verbiage.

Dulles then embarked on what he melodramatically described as a "policy of massive retaliation" or "brinkmanship," the essence of which was that this country would go "to the very brink of war" to prevent the further spread of Communism. But this policy too was found wanting when in 1954 the French abandoned much of Indochina in Southeast Asia to Communist forces under Ho Chi Minh, the present ruler of North Vietnam. Prior to the French retreat, Dulles had announced that Indochina was the key to all Southeast Asia and must be kept in the free world at any cost. After the French defeat, he muttered something to the effect that Indochina's strategic value had been "overrated." At a later date the United States intervened in Southeast Asia to the extent of providing military and other foreign aid to non-Communist Thailand and South Vietnam, but the policy of brinkmanship was put aside as impractical.

After Secretary Dulles's death, Eisenhower shifted to a more conciliatory position, letting it be known that the United States would be willing at any time to negotiate with the Soviet Union to seek ways to relieve international tensions. Simultaneously the free world suffered a serious setback in the cold war with the establishment in Cuba, only ninety miles off the American mainland, of a Communist government under Fidel Castro.

Such, in a general way, was the status of the cold war when in January of 1961 hordes of visitors began pouring into Washington, D.C., to witness the induction into office of the youngest man ever elected President of the United States, forty-three-year-old John Fitzgerald Kennedy of Massachusetts.

9

"I am not the Catholic candidate for President"

☆ ☆ ☆

JOHN F. KENNEDY

Not since the days of Theodore Roosevelt had so many glittering special events been scheduled for a presidential inauguration. And not since William Howard Taft had Mother Nature shown more indifference to the plans of inauguration committees.

In 1961 the great event fell on a Friday. On the previous Monday, messages began dribbling in from the offices of the United States Weather Bureau hinting of unpleasant conditions ahead. The reality, when it struck, far exceeded the forecasts. On Thursday afternoon a southwest wind roared into Washington, bringing with it a fine, stinging snow that by nightfall had reached the height of 6 inches and by the following morning an almost unprecedented 7.7 inches.

Those familiar with the big and handsome capital city are aware that its somewhat southerly-oriented inhabitants have been known to panic at the sight of a snowflake. With a million inauguration visitors in town, the effects of the sleet-like downpour that Thursday afternoon were indescribable.

By midafternoon authorities were designating the traffic jam in downtown Washington as "absolutely hopeless." Thousands of employees, pouring from the asbestos-sided temporary buildings and marble mausoleums where the wheels of government go 'round, were unable to find their automobiles or to move them if they found them. At every bus and trolley stop, scantily clad government girls shivered in the howling wind as they waited for transportation that couldn't get there. Her high-spiked heels lost from view in the powdery underfooting, one young lady was heard to lament, "It seems that in this town almost nobody ever dresses for the weather until it gets here."

Three thousand men, 500 trucks, and 200 snowplows were soon in action. All night long, a special component of a hundred snowplows and thirty cranes was kept busy clearing the parade route of 1,500 stranded cars.

With the National Airport closed, scores of dignitaries coming from all over the world were either unable to reach the city or compelled to do so by roundabout routes. The plane winging from New York with Adlai Stevenson, soon to be his country's Ambassador to the United Nations, was forced to land at Byrd Field in Richmond, Virginia. From there the Ambassador-designate and his party traveled northward by car over ninety miles of slippery and at points dangerously drifted highways. The plane bringing former

President Herbert Hoover from Florida circled the snow-bound Washington airport and sped back to Miami, whence eighty-seven-year-old Hoover telegraphed his apologies to the President-elect.

Retiring President Eisenhower looked through the White House windows, shook his head, and put in a telephone call to 3307 N Street Northwest, the President-elect's home in the Georgetown area of Washington. The President suggested that in view of the weather Kennedy and his wife call at the White House sufficiently early the next morning to share a cup of coffee with the Eisenhowers before they started their trek to the Capitol. Kennedy accepted the invitation with thanks, and the President put in two more calls, issuing the same invitation to Vice President and Mrs. Richard Nixon and to Vice President-elect and Mrs. Lyndon Johnson.

Meanwhile, in Georgetown, the President-elect and his charming wife Jacqueline were making preparations for a busy evening. Some of the pre-inauguration events had been canceled, but two were to take place: the concert at Constitution Hall in the early evening and the big gala under the direction of Hollywood singing star Frank Sinatra at the Armory at a later hour.

With the inrush of the first snowflakes shortly after noon, the Kennedys had sent their white Lincoln sedan to a nearby filling station to have chains put on. As darkness arrived with no sign of car or driver, Kennedy decided to exercise his presidential prerogatives a day in advance. Calling the White House garage, he requested a limousine.

When shortly after seven the Kennedys left home, a Secret Service man held an umbrella for Jacqueline as she and her husband made a dash for the waiting car. Mrs. Kennedy, whose exquisite taste in clothes was to place its stamp on the American fashion world for years to come, was wearing a simple white dress of heavy stiff silk, a choker of emeralds and diamonds, and matching pendant earrings. No wrap protected her trim figure.

Several blocks from the house, the slowly moving limousine was met by a motorcycle convoy. Thereafter, progress was swifter. Even so, it was 8:07 p.m., an hour after their departure from close-by Georgetown, when the Kennedys reached Constitution Hall.

Others had far more trouble. It took the newly designated Secretary of State Dean Rusk and his wife an hour and twenty minutes to reach the Hall from the Statler Hotel, only a few blocks away. Walking from another downtown hotel, the conductor of the National Symphony Orchestra, Howard Mitchell, arrived fifteen minutes after the Kennedys. Forty members of his one-hundred-piece orchestra never did arrive, and half of the 3,800 seats of a sold-out house remained empty throughout the performance.

At 9:16 the Kennedys left the concert to drive to the Washington Armory on the eastern outskirts of the city. Although the gala prepared by Sinatra was an hour and forty minutes late in getting started, it turned out to be a lavish and enjoyable variety show. Mahalia Jackson sang "The Star-Spangled Banner." Ethel Merman belted out "Everything's Coming Up Roses"—to the amusement of associates aware that she was a staunch Republican. Frederic March read the farewell address given by Lincoln to his Springfield neighbors as he left them to journey to Washington for his own first inauguration. Other personalities of the entertainment world taking part in the two-and-a-half-hour spectacle were Nat King Cole, Ella Fitzgerald, Sir Laurence Olivier, Helen Traubel, Tony Curtis, and Janet Leigh.

☆ ☆ ☆

The snow ceased falling during the night. Participants in the inauguration of the thirty-fourth President[1] will always remember Friday, January 20, 1961, as a day of blinding-bright sun and a nippy wind that kept the thermometer well below the freezing mark.

At 8 a.m. the President-elect sat down for breakfast at his Georgetown home. At 8:55 he left for a short time to attend Mass at nearby Holy Trinity Church. When two hours later he and Jacqueline emerged from the house to begin their ride to the White House, five hundred neighbors were on hand to cheer them off.

Hatless and coatless, seventy-year-old Eisenhower was waiting for them on the north portico of the White House. Reporters described as "unusually cordial" the exchange of greetings between the oldest man ever to occupy the Presidency and the youngest ever elected to it.

Of the six cars making up the cavalcade to the Capitol twenty-five minutes later, two were occupied by Secret Service agents. Eisenhower and Kennedy rode in the lead car. Their wives were in the fourth car; the retiring and incoming Vice Presidents were in the fifth car; and their wives were in the car behind them.

Technically, the President should take his oath at noon,

[1] Thirty-fifth if you count Grover Cleveland, whose two terms were divided, as two.

but as far as the records show, no swearing-in ceremony has ever started on time except for Thomas Jefferson's. The members of Kennedy's party arrived at the Capitol well in advance of the appointed hour, but their progress to the platform above the steps of the east portico was impeded by hundreds of autograph-seekers and individuals determined to shake the hands of "Ike" and "Jack." There was a further delay when the discovery was made that there were not enough chairs on the platform, and additional ones had to be rushed out from the Capitol.

It was nine minutes after noon when Eisenhower stepped on to the platform to hear the Marine Band play "Hail to the Chief" in his honor for the last time. When Kennedy joined him a few minutes later, the two men, seated side by side behind the lectern, doffed their silk hats and engaged in animated conversation.

Among those sitting with them in the front row were the parents of the President-elect, Mr. and Mrs. Joseph P. Kennedy of Boston, and several other members of his large family. All the Kennedy women wore mink coats except Jacqueline, whose fawn-colored cloth coat was touched with sable and whose white-gloved hands were tucked into a brown muff of the same material.

Among the many dignitaries on the platform were former President Harry S. Truman and his wife and the widow of Woodrow Wilson. Franklin Roosevelt's widow was out front in a section reserved for the diplomatic corps. Mrs. Eleanor Roosevelt had expressed a preference for sitting where she could see "the faces rather than the backs" of the speakers. On the platform, electric heaters along the base of the front railing took the edge off the 22-degree temperature.

The 50,000 people assembled in front of the platform fell silent as Senator John Sparkman of Alabama, chairman of the Joint Congressional Inaugural Committee, appeared at the lectern and called on the band to open the ceremony with "America the Beautiful."

Sparkman was succeeded by Richard Cardinal Cushing, Catholic Archbishop of Boston, whose invocation was so long that a subsequent inaugural committee would write a time limit on prayers into the directives for the 1965 ceremonies for President Johnson.

Barely had the stately prelate started speaking when wisps of smoke began pouring from the lectern, bringing expressions of consternation to the faces of the Secret Service men at the rear of the platform. As the Cardinal, seemingly unperturbed, continued with his ten-minute prayer, irreverent wags in the audience speculated in whispers that either the good Lord was displeased with the length of the invocation or the Devil was demanding equal time. When the Cardinal had finished, the relieved Secret Service agents rapidly doused what turned out to be a blaze in the electrical apparatus attached in Franklin Roosevelt's day to make it possible to adjust the height of the lectern.

The emergency disposed of, the famous contralto Marian Anderson sang "The Star-Spangled Banner." Reporters noted that as Miss Anderson was singing, the President-elect mouthed the words of the National Anthem with her, apparently experiencing no difficulty in recalling the little-known second stanza.

Next came a shorter prayer by Archbishop Iakovos of the Greek Orthodox Church. Then Lyndon B. Johnson stepped forward and was sworn in as Vice President, with his friend and fellow Texan, Speaker Sam Rayburn of the House of Representatives, administering the oath. This phase of the proceedings was followed by a third prayer from the Reverend Dr. John Barclay, pastor of the Central Christian Church of Austin, Texas.

Now came a touching moment as America's unofficial poet laureate, Robert Frost, approached the lectern. The appearance of a creative writer on the presidential swearing-in platform was an innovation to which the newspapers and magazines of the world had devoted thousands of words during the preceding weeks.

Frost's presence marked the first time a President-elect had seized on his inauguration as an opportunity to honor his country's contributors to the arts and sciences. The decision to do so had been made during the last month of the preceding year, when Kennedy had extended a special invitation to attend the inauguration to 155 American writers, artists, scientists, poets, philosophers, and composers of music. In addition, he had sent a telegram to the little town of Derry, New Hampshire, asking Robert Frost to participate in the ceremonies by reading a poem.

Eighty-six-year-old Frost's reply had been in the classic vein of his work. "If you can bear at your age the honor of being made President of the United States," he wired the young man about to assume the burdens of the White House, "I ought to be able at my age to bear the honor of taking some part in your inauguration."

And now the aged poet was standing at the lectern on the presidential platform, his white hair whipping in the eighteen-mile-an-hour breeze. Originally Kennedy had suggested that he prepare a special poem for the occasion. To this the New England author had demurred. "Occasional poetry," he said, "is not my style." Subsequently the President-elect had suggested that Frost read "The Gift Outright," a poem written in 1930 and published as part of a 1942 volume entitled *A Witness Tree.*

What the poet had prepared for the inauguration was a rhymed preface dedicating his poem to the President-to-be. He had inserted a copy of the preface in the book he brought to the speaking stand, but his efforts to read it were defeated by the brilliance of the sun flashing up from the whitened earth below him and from the marble of the recently extended front walls of the central portion of the Capitol behind him. "I can't see in the sun," he was heard to mutter.

Vice President Johnson, hastening forward, held his top hat above the lectern in an attempt to shade the poet's manuscript. Frost shook his head, saying that although he could not read his dedication he could present his poem because he knew it by heart.

In a firm baritone he then recited the sixteen-line, unrhymed but strictly metered poem the gist of which was that the beautiful land given to the American people did not really become theirs until they sprinkled its soil with their blood in the American Revolution and bestowed their loyalty on the nation thus created—

The land was ours before we were the land's.
She was our land more than a hundred years
Before we were her people. She was ours
In Massachusetts, in Virginia.
But we were England's, still colonials,
Possessing what we still were unpossessed by,

Possessed by what we now no more possessed.
Something we were withholding made us weak
Until we found out that it was ourselves
We were withholding from our land of living,
And forthwith found salvation in surrender.
Such as we were we gave ourselves outright
(The deed of gift was many deeds of war)
To the land vaguely realizing westward,
But still unstoried, artless, unenhanced,
Such as she was, such as she will become.

At the time of its first publication, the last phrase of the poem had read "such as she *would* become." Frost had changed it in deference to the wishes of the President-elect, who, as the poet explained, "wants to say 'will' because it is in the four years ahead that he is going to do something here. . . ."

☆ ☆ ☆

At 12:51 p.m., John Fitzgerald Kennedy repeated the words of the oath after Chief Justice Earl Warren, added "So help me, God," and began his short but eloquent inaugural address.

He called for "a grand and global alliance" to combat "tyranny, poverty, disease and war." He served notice that under his leadership the United States would stand ready "to pay any price" to assure the survival and "the success of liberty." At the same time, he said, his administration would be ready to sit down at the conference table at any time with the leaders of the Soviet Union. "Let us never negotiate out of fear," was the theme of this section of his address, "but let us never fear to negotiate."

So began the administration that was to be so tragically

cut short only two years and nine months later by the bullet of an assassin. Fresh in the memories of millions of Americans are its major highlights.

During the 1960 election campaign, the then United States Senator had been severely critical of Eisenhower for what Kennedy believed to be the Republican President's failure to make sufficient effort to uproot the recently established Communist government in Cuba. On taking office, however, Kennedy discovered that detailed plans to this end had been drawn up by the Eisenhower administration.

The plans called for an American-supported invasion of Cuba by a small band of anti-Castro Cubans. Its stated objective was to stir up within Cuba a revolution that would topple the Castro regime and replace it by a more democratic government.

After weeks of anxious conference with his aides, Kennedy decided to make use of the Eisenhower invasion plans, with certain modifications. Put into effect in the early morning hours of April 17, 1961, however, the invasion turned out to be an abject failure. To what extent the outcome was due to incorrect advice on the part of Kennedy's aides; to what extent it was due to his own lack of experience—these questions are still hotly and widely debated and no doubt will be for years to come.

In the late autumn of 1962, Cuba was back in the news with the revelation that the Soviet Union was installing on the island a number of offensive missile and bomber bases capable of nuclear attack on the mainland of the United States.

The President who rose to cope with this challenge was a far tougher man than the President who had fumbled the invasion attempt of the year before. By a proclamation issued on October 24, 1962, he placed a naval "quarantine" around Cuba and announced that any Soviet vessels found bringing nuclear armaments to the island would be stopped by American warships and turned back.

The threat of a third world war and possible nuclear disaster hung over the world until the following October 27, when Chairman Khrushchev, the Russian leader, pledged that his country would stop work on the Cuban bases, dismantle the missiles already there, and return them to the Soviet Union. Kennedy's failure, later, to achieve an on-the-ground inspection of the dismantled Cuban missile sites was much criticized, but the consensus both in the United States and abroad was that in one of the gravest crises of the twentieth century the young President had acted with fortitude and wise restraint.

Still another achievement of the Kennedy administration was put on record not quite a year later when the United States Senate ratified a treaty with Russia banning the testing above ground of dangerous high-yield nuclear bombs. The ratification of the limited test ban marked the first real "thaw" in the cold war since its inception. It did not, of course, put an end to the tensions created by a divided world. These were still very much with us when on November 22, 1963, John Kennedy died on the operating table of a hospital in Dallas, Texas.

☆ ☆ ☆

Far too little time has elapsed for students of American government to subject Kennedy's contributions to his office and nation to the careful appraisal that the administrations of most of his predecessors have received. It is certain that the American people will always warmly remember their witty and personable young Chief Executive. It is also certain that future historians will make emphatic note of the role played by his election campaign in putting an end to an old and undemocratic American prejudice.

Subsequent to the defeat of Al Smith in the election of 1928, it had become an axiom of American politics that it would be many generations before a Roman Catholic would even hope to occupy the White House. The victory of Catholic Kennedy put the quietus to this assumption. The 1960 election was close; the Democratic contender received only 112,881 more popular votes than his Republican opponent, Richard Nixon.

After it was over, numerous political observers concluded that one of the reasons for Kennedy's victory was the manner in which he had handled the religious issue. Unquestionably, future Americans will have many occasions to remember his sensible remarks on the subject in one of his major election-campaign speeches—a speech delivered on September 12, 1960, before a meeting of the Greater Houston Ministerial Association in Texas.

"I am not the Catholic candidate for President," Senator Kennedy told his Protestant audience that evening. "I am the Democratic Party's candidate for President who happens to be a Catholic.

> *I do not speak for my church* [he went on] *on public matters—and the church does not speak for me. Whatever issue may come before me as President, if elected, I will make my decision in accordance with . . . what my conscience tells me to be in the national*

interest and without regard to outside religious pressure or dictate.

[I]f the time should ever come . . . when my office would require me either to violate my conscience or violate the national interest, then I would resign the office, and I hope any other conscientious public servant would do likewise.

But I do not intend to . . . disavow either my views or my church in order to win this election. If I should lose on the real issues, I shall return to my seat in the Senate satisfied that I tried my best and was fairly judged.

But if this election is decided on the basis that forty million [Catholic] Americans lost their chance of being President on the day they were baptized, then it is the whole nation that will be the loser in the eyes of Catholics and non-Catholics around the world, in the eyes of history, and in the eyes of our own people.

Bibliography

So far as I've been able to discover, the only books dealing exclusively with the presidential inauguration are Glen D. Kittler's *Hail to the Chief*, published in Philadelphia in 1965, Emil Edward Hurja's *History of Presidential Inaugurations*, a Democratic campaign document published in New York in 1933, and Thomas H. McKee's *Presidential Inaugurations from George Washington . . . to Grover Cleveland . . .*, published in Washington in 1893.

Of much help in the preparation of this account of the great ceremony has been the bibliography assembled by the Library of Congress and published by the Government Printing Office. Entitled *Presidential Inauguration, A Selected List of References*, the 1960 revised edition provides hundreds of references to books, government documents, newspapers, and periodicals. Available at the Library of Congress itself is a mimeographed supplement to the bibliography, dated October 27, 1964, and compiled by Carolyn M. Holland.

The items given below include some of the more useful references suggested by the Library of Congress, along with other publications pertinent to the inauguration as an institution, to individual inaugurations, to the Presidency as an institution, to individual Presidents, and to the three cities —New York, Philadelphia, and Washington—where all the regularly elected Presidents have been sworn in.

Ackman, Lonnelle, *We, the People: The Story of the U. S. Capitol, Its Past and Its Promise*, 1963.

Adams, Katherine H., "Famous Inaugurations," *Forward*, Vol. 48 (July 20, 1929), p. 226.

"Apropos Inaugurals," *Musical America*, Vol. 81 (March, 1961), p. 29.

Austen, Albert A., "The 'Traditional' Presidential Inaugural Address," in Kirk, Rudolph, and C. F. Main, eds., *Essays in Literary History* . . . New Brunswick, N. J., 1960.

Baker, Abby G., "Inauguration Day at the National Capital," *Woman's Home Companion*, Vol. 32 (March, 1905), p. 52ff.

Bankers Trust Company, N.Y., *Wall and Nassau: An Account of the Inauguration of George Washington* . . . New York, 1939.

"Behind the Inaugural Mike," *Newsweek*, Vol. 33 (January 31, 1949), p. 49.

Bernard, Kenneth A., "Lincoln and the Music of the Civil War," *Lincoln Herald*, Spring 1961, pp. 29-35.

Bishop, Joseph Bucklin, *Our Political Drama, Conventions, Campaigns, Candidates; with numerous . . . reproductions of caricatures*. New York, 1904.

Borden, Morton, ed., *America's Ten Greatest Presidents*. Chicago, 1961.

Brant, Theron L., "The Fourth of March: The Drama of Our Presidential Inaugurations." *Everybody's Magazine*, Vol. 12 (March, 1905), pp. 371-6.

Burns, James MacGregor, *Roosevelt: The Lion and the Fox*. New York, 1956.

Caemmerer, Hans Paul, A *Manual on the Origin and Development of Washington*. 75th Congress, 3d Session, Senate Document No. 178, 1939.

Corwin, Edward Samuel, and Louis William Koenig, *The Presidency Today*. New York, 1956.

Crowningshield, Mrs. Schuyler, "The Inauguration Ball at Washington." *Delineator*, Vol. 57 (May, 1901), pp. 803-8.

Cuthbert, Norma Barrett, ed., *Lincoln and the Baltimore Plot, 1861, from Pinkerton Records and Related Papers*. San Marino, Calif., 1949.

Dos Passos, John, *The Head and Heart of Thomas Jefferson*. New York, 1954.

Dowe, Charles E., "The Inauguration of the First President." *Cosmopolitan*, Vol. 6 (April, 1889), pp. 533-43.

Eckenrode, Hamilton James, *Rutherford B. Hayes: Statesman of Reunion*. Port Washington, N.Y., 1963.

Eiselen, Malcom R., "Preserve, Protect and Defend—" *North American Review*, Winter 1936-37, pp. 334-49.

"Epic of America Written in Its Inaugurals." *The New York Times Magazine*, January 17, 1937, pp. 14-15.

"The 44th Inaugural." *Newsweek*, Vol. 57 (January 30, 1961), pp. 18-19.

Freeman, Douglas Southall, *George Washington: A Biography*, 7 vols. New York, 1948-1956.

Fuller, Helen, *Year of Trial: Kennedy's Crucial Decisions*. New York, 1962.

Garraty, John A., *Woodrow Wilson: A Great Life in Brief*. New York, 1956.

Graham, A. P., and M. Fuller, "Inaugural Firsts." *American Mercury*, Vol. 60 (February, 1945), pp. 169-73.

Handlin, Oscar, ed., *American Principles and Issues: The National Purpose*. New York, 1961.

Hitchcock, F. H., "The Inauguration" (T.R.'s second). *Harper's Weekly*, Vol. 49 (March 4, 1905), pp. 304-06.

Hoffman, Jay K., "From 1789 to 1961, Inaugural Music since Washington's Day." *The New York Times*, January 15, 1961, pp. x-9.

Hunt, Gaillard, "The First Inauguration Ball." *Century Magazine*, Vol. 69 (March, 1905), pp. 754-60.

Hyman, Sidney, *The American President*. New York, 1954.

173

"The Inauguration Ball from Madison to McKinley." *Harper's Weekly*, Vol. 41 (March 13, 1897), p. 262ff.

Johnson, Gerald W., "Nine Inaugurations, Nine Turning Points." *The New York Times Magazine*, January 18, 1953. pp. 8-9, 40.

Jones, Dorothea, and Stuart E. Jones, "Pennsylvania Avenue, Route of Presidents . . ." *National Geographic* Magazine, Vol. 111 (January, 1957), pp. 63-95.

Kean, Charles D., "Epiphany Bells." *Christian Century*, Vol. 78 (February 1, 1961), p. 158.

Leech, Margaret, *Reveille in Washington, 1860-1865*. New York, 1941.

Life editors, *Inaugural Spectacle*. Souvenir edition, 1961.

McKelway, A. J., "President Wilson, His Inauguration, Cabinet and Problems." *Outlook*, Vol. 103 (March 15, 1913).

Miers, Earl Schenck, ed., *Lincoln Day by Day, A Chronology, 1809-1865*. Vol. III: 1861-1865. Washington, 1960.

Moore, Barbara, "When Presidents Take Office." *American Heritage*, Vol. 4 (Spring 1953), pp. 5-7.

Morris, Richard B., *Encyclopedia of American History*, revised and enlarged. New York, 1960.

Pearce, Mrs. John N., and William V. Elder III, *The White House, an Historic Guide*, 1963.

Pringle, Harry E., *Theodore Roosevelt*, rev. ed. New York, 1956.

Roseboom, Eugene H., *A History of Presidential Elections*. New York, 1964.

Rossiter, Clinton L., *The American Presidency*, rev. ed. New York, 1963.

Sandburg, Carl, *Address Upon the Occasion of Abraham Lincoln's 100th Inaugural Anniversary*. . . . Chicago, 1961.

Schachner, Nathan, *The Founding Fathers*. New York, 1954.

Scherf, Carl, "Slang, Slogan and Song in American Politics." *Social Studies*, Vol. 25, No. 8 (December, 1934).

Schlesinger, Arthur M., Jr., *The Age of Jackson*. Boston, 1948.

——, *The Crisis of the Old Order, 1919-1933* (Vol. I of *The Age of Roosevelt*). Boston, 1957.

——, *The Coming of the New Deal* (Vol. II of *The Age of Roosevelt*). Boston, 1959.

Shapiro, Harvey, "Story of the Poem" (Interview with Robert Frost). *The New York Times Magazine*, January 15, 1961, pp. 6, 86.

174

Stampp, Kenneth Milton, *The Era of Reconstruction, 1865-77*. New York, 1965.

Thach, Charles C., The Creation of the Presidency, 1775-1789." *Johns Hopkins University Studies*, Series 40, No. 4. Baltimore, 1922.

Thomas, Benjamin P., *Abraham Lincoln, a Biography*. New York, 1952.

U. S. Congress . . . House Document No. 523. *Ceremonies and Re-enactment of the First Inauguration of Abraham Lincoln, 1861-1961*. . . . Washington, 1962.

Van Doren, Carl, *The Great Rehearsal*. New York, 1948.

Washington Post Potomac. 1965 Inaugural Edition.

Wharton, Anne H. "Washington's New York Residence in 1789." *Lippincott's Monthly Magazine*, Vol. 43 (1889), pp. 741-5.

BLANK

BLANK

PAGES 181
182 } BLANK PAGES

180